SURREALIST
PHOTOGRAPHY
COLLECTION

STEAL ADCOCK, M.A., LPC

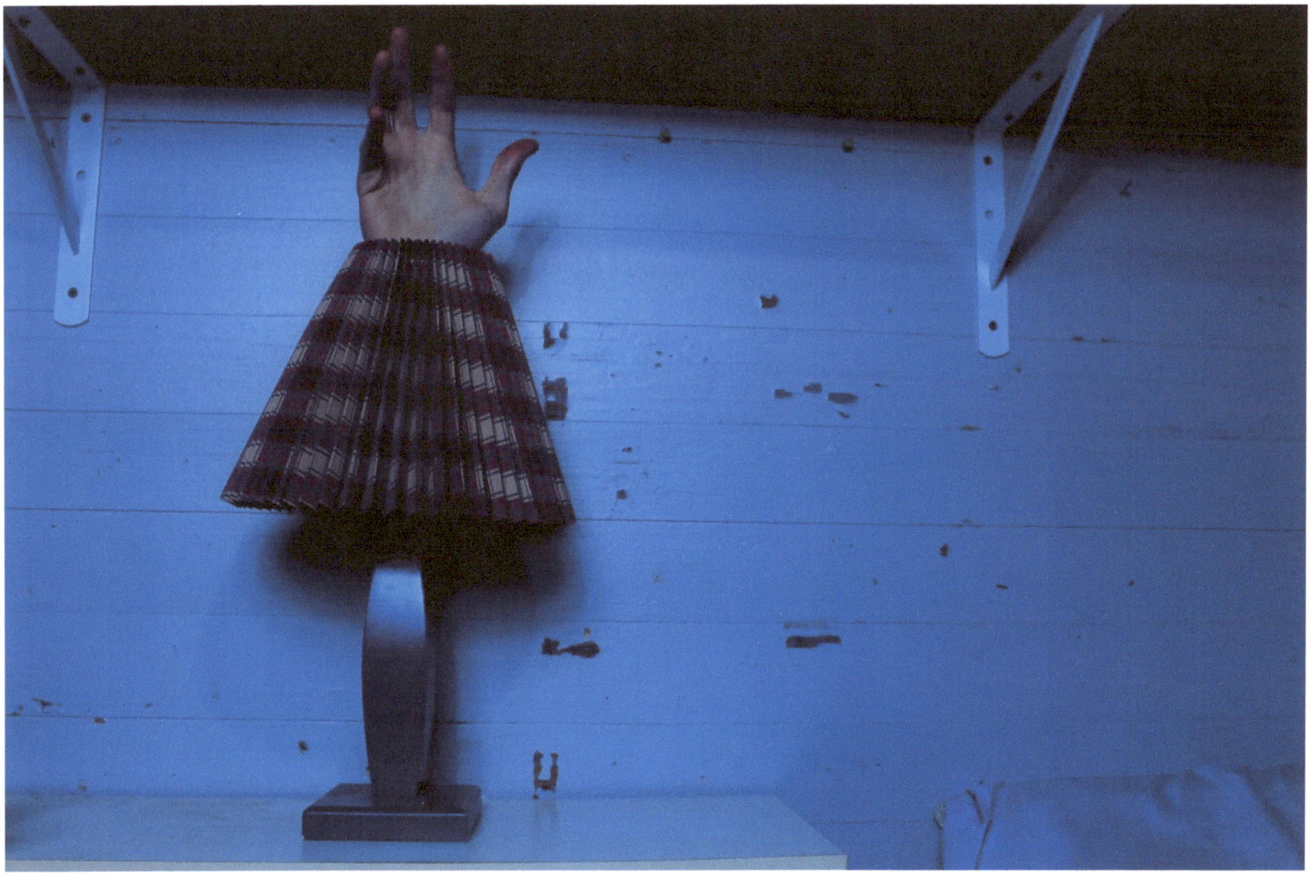

SURREALIST PHOTOGRAPHY COLLECTION

ALL PHOTOS BY: STEAL ADCOCK, M.A., LPC

Contents

Dreams

Nightmares

Visions

Illusions

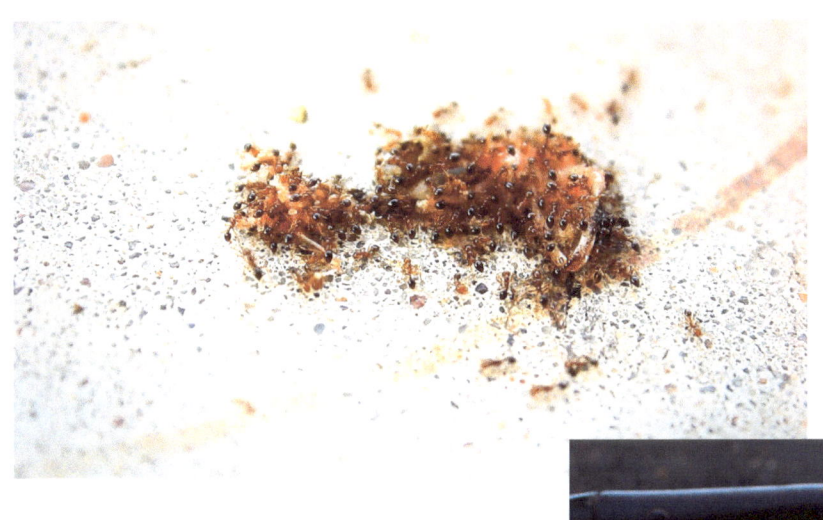

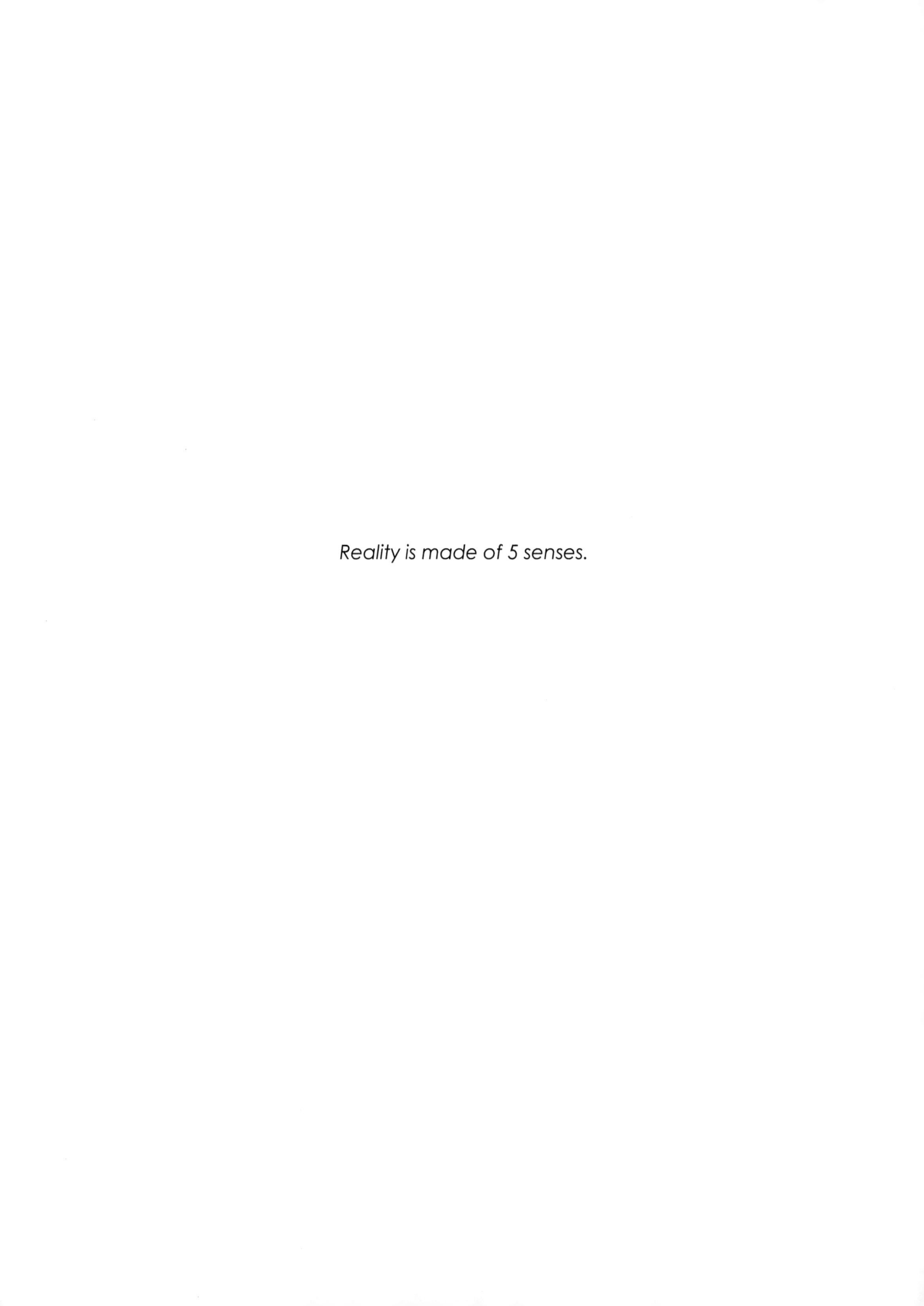

Reality is made of 5 senses.

Dreams.

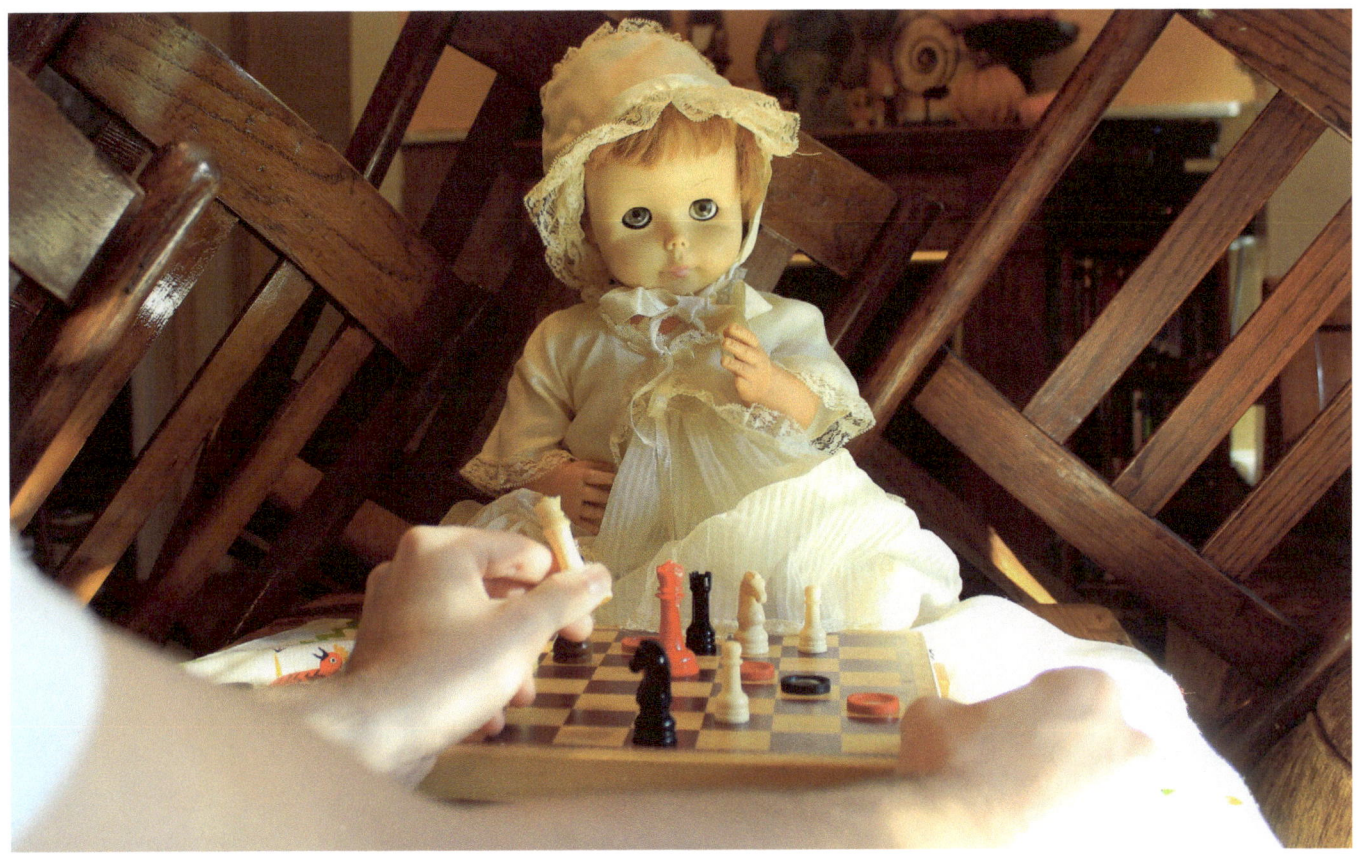

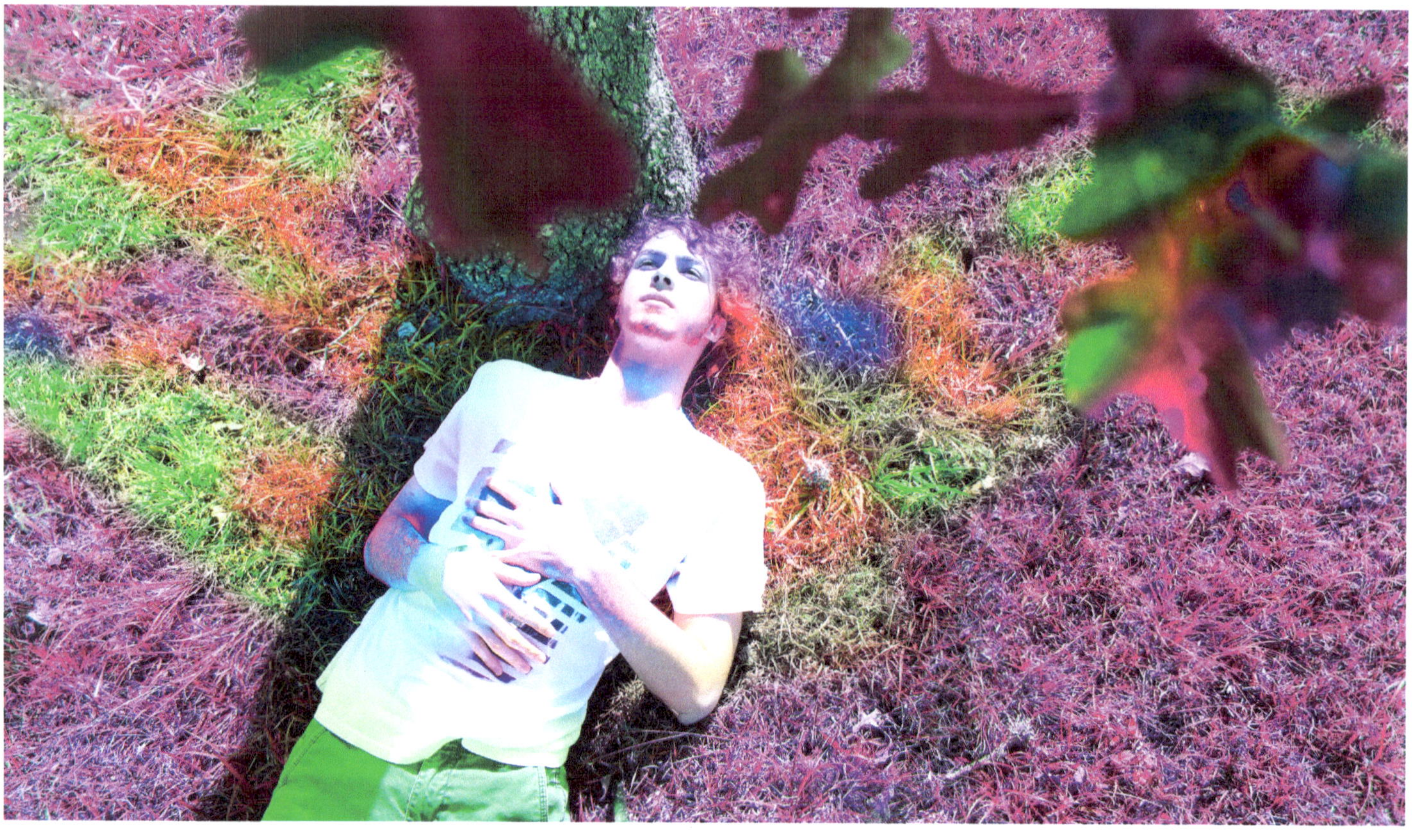

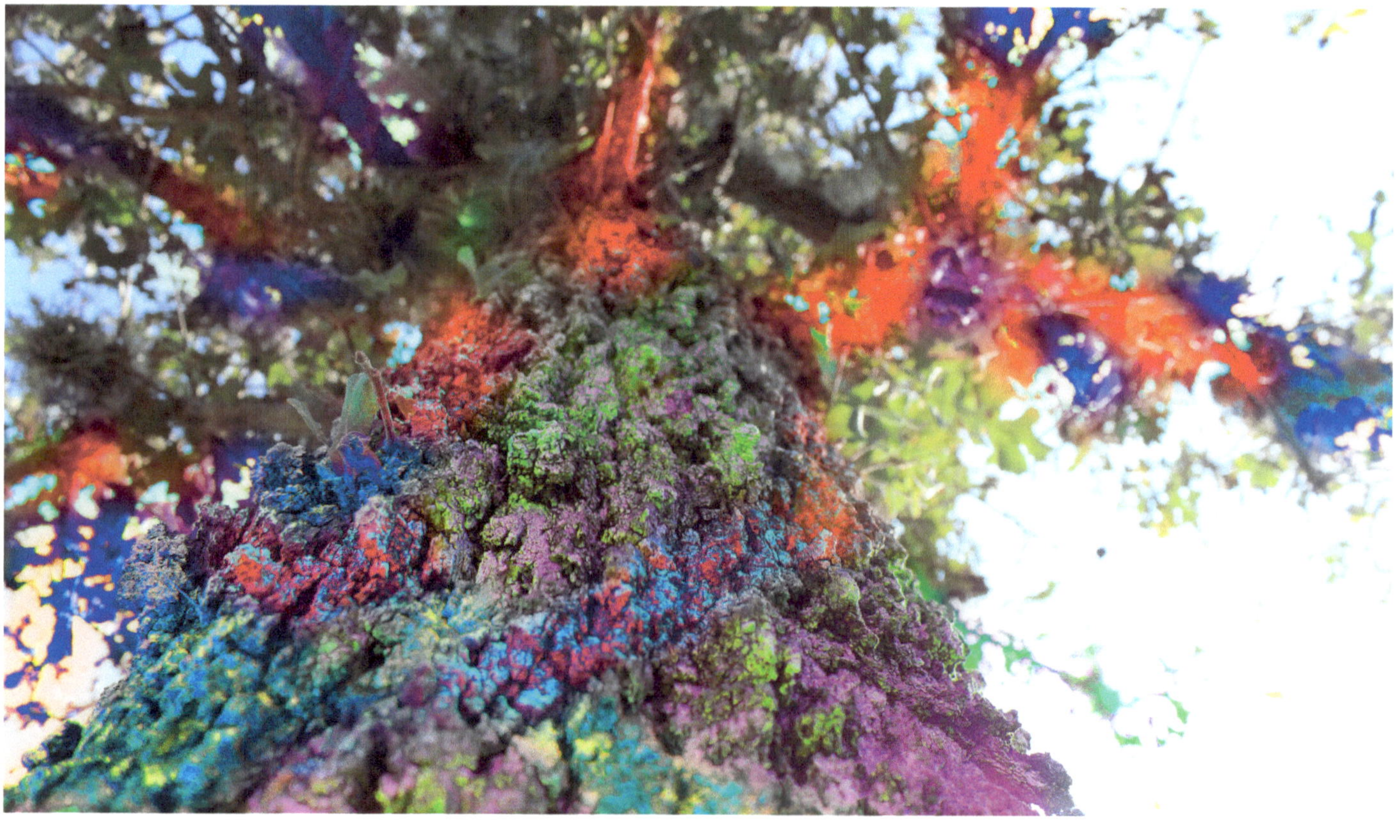

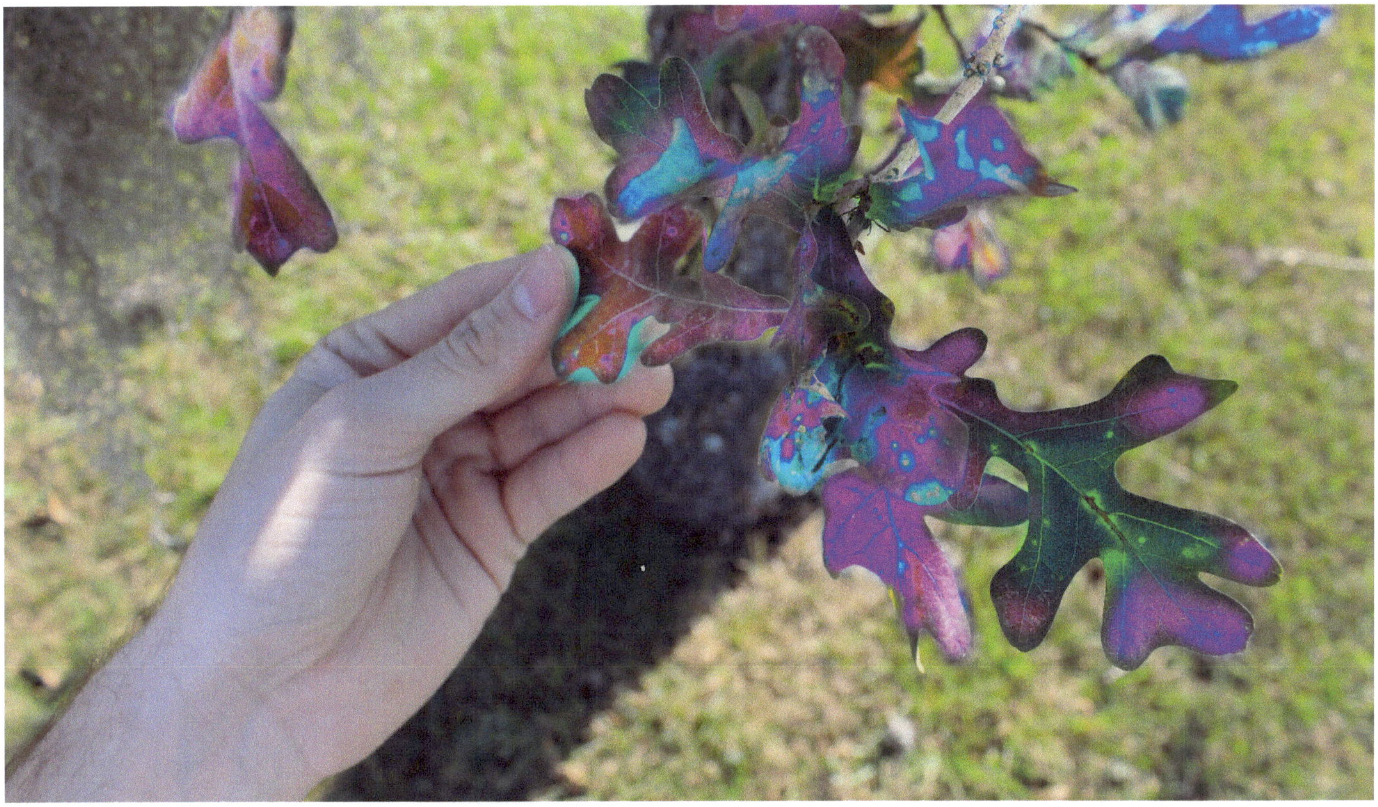

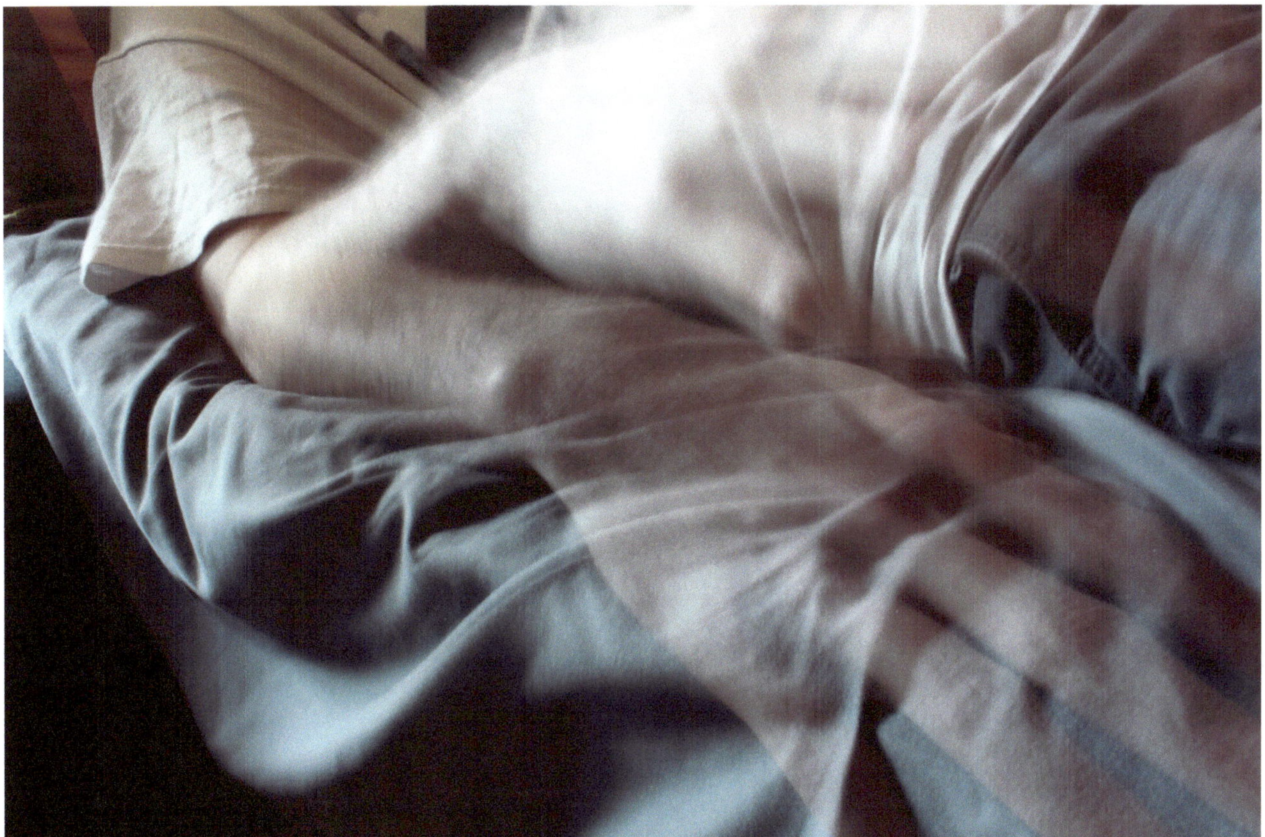

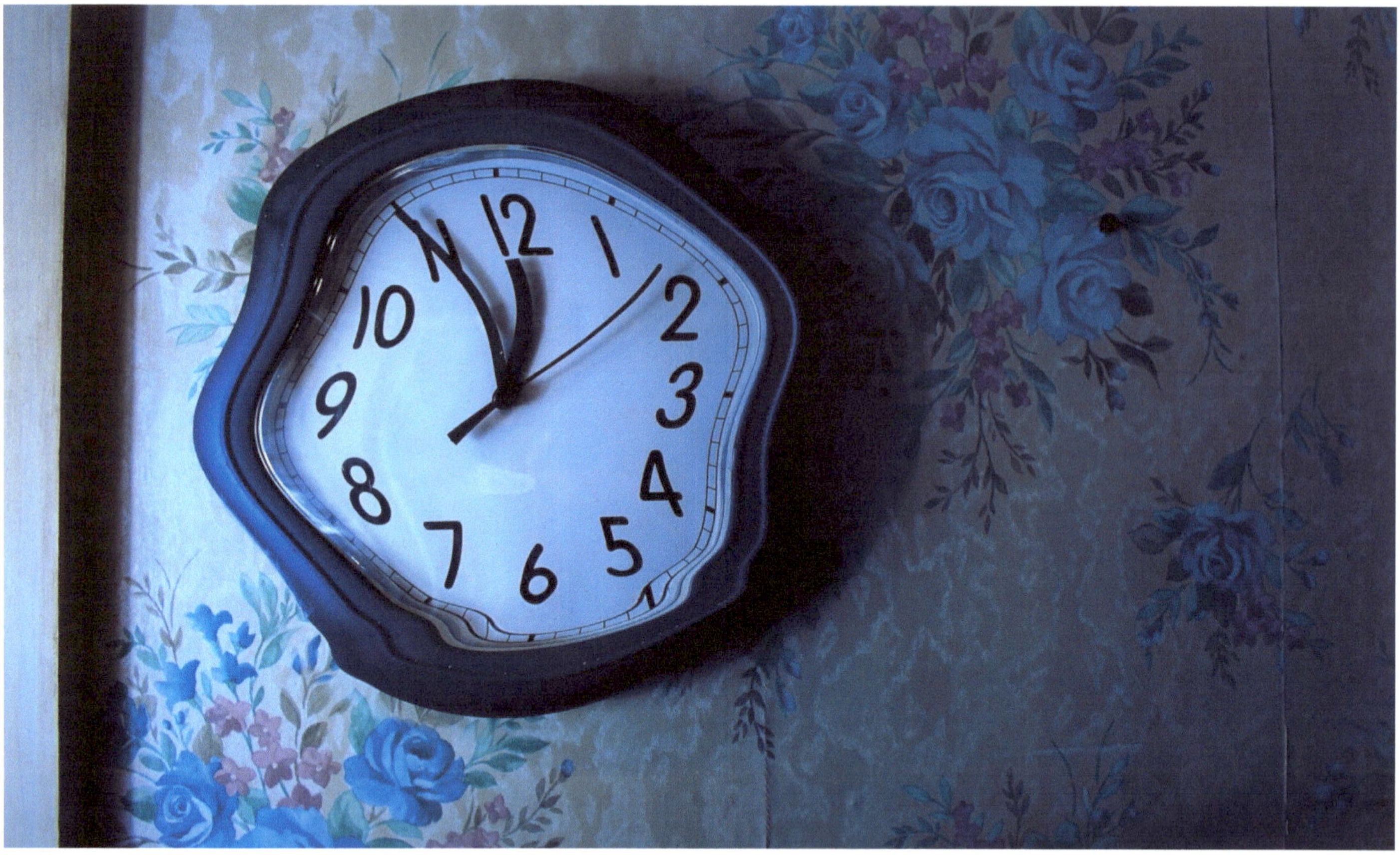

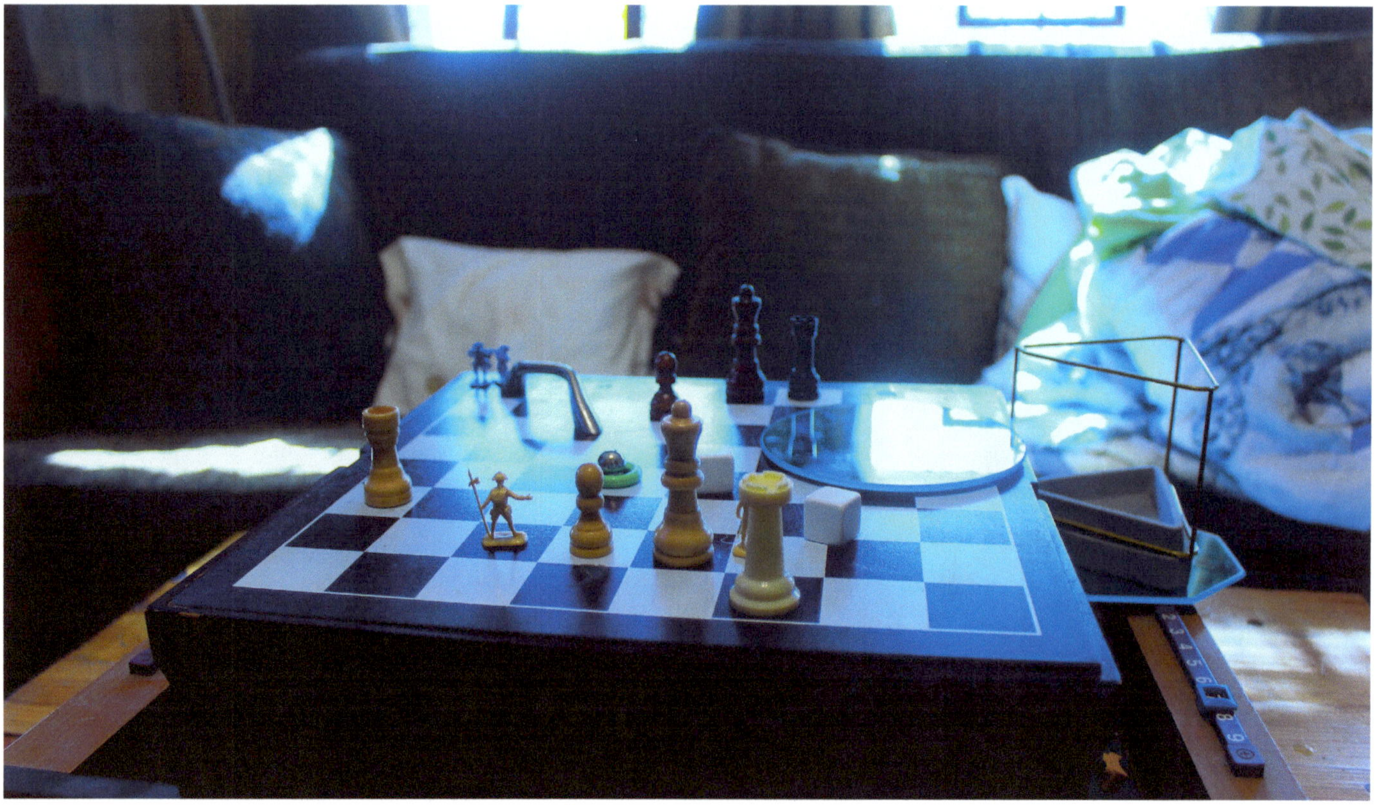

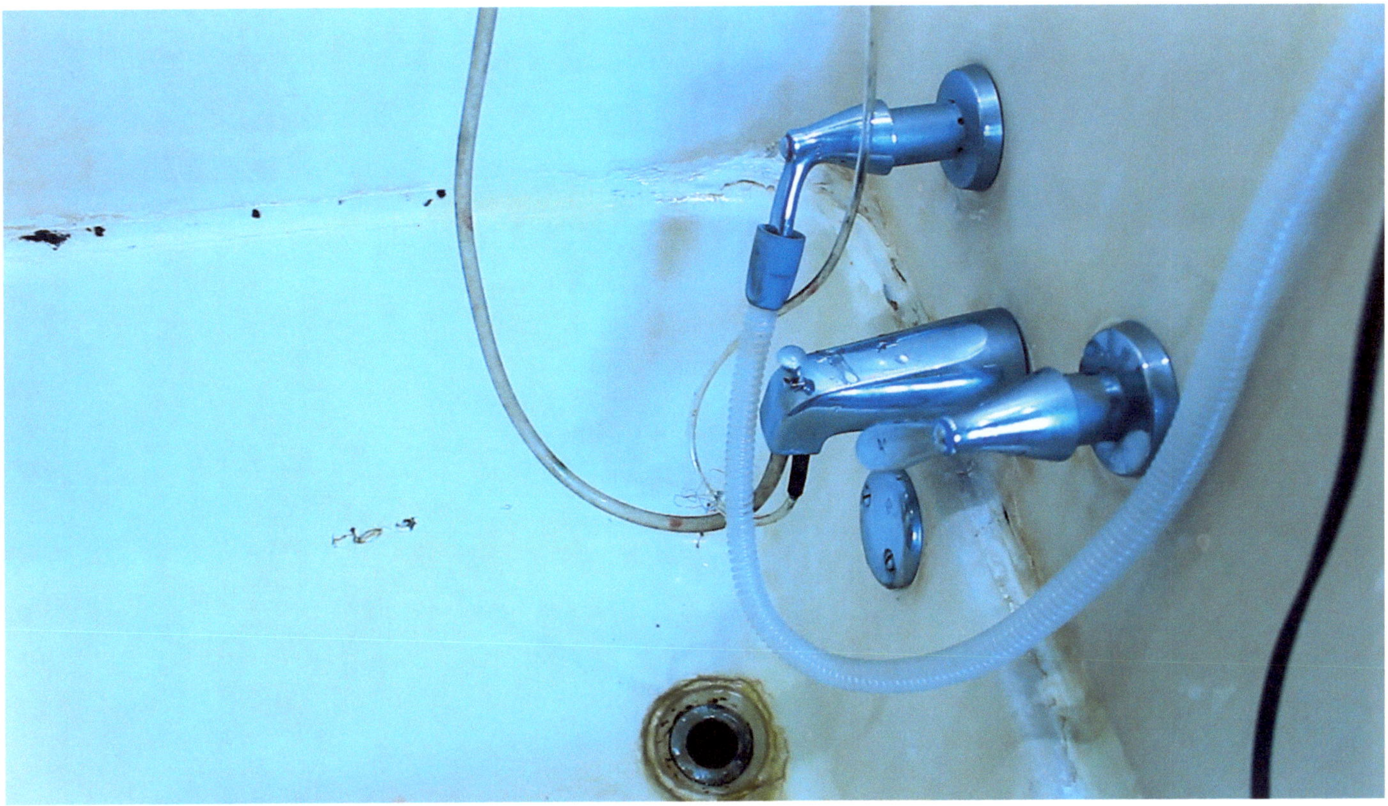

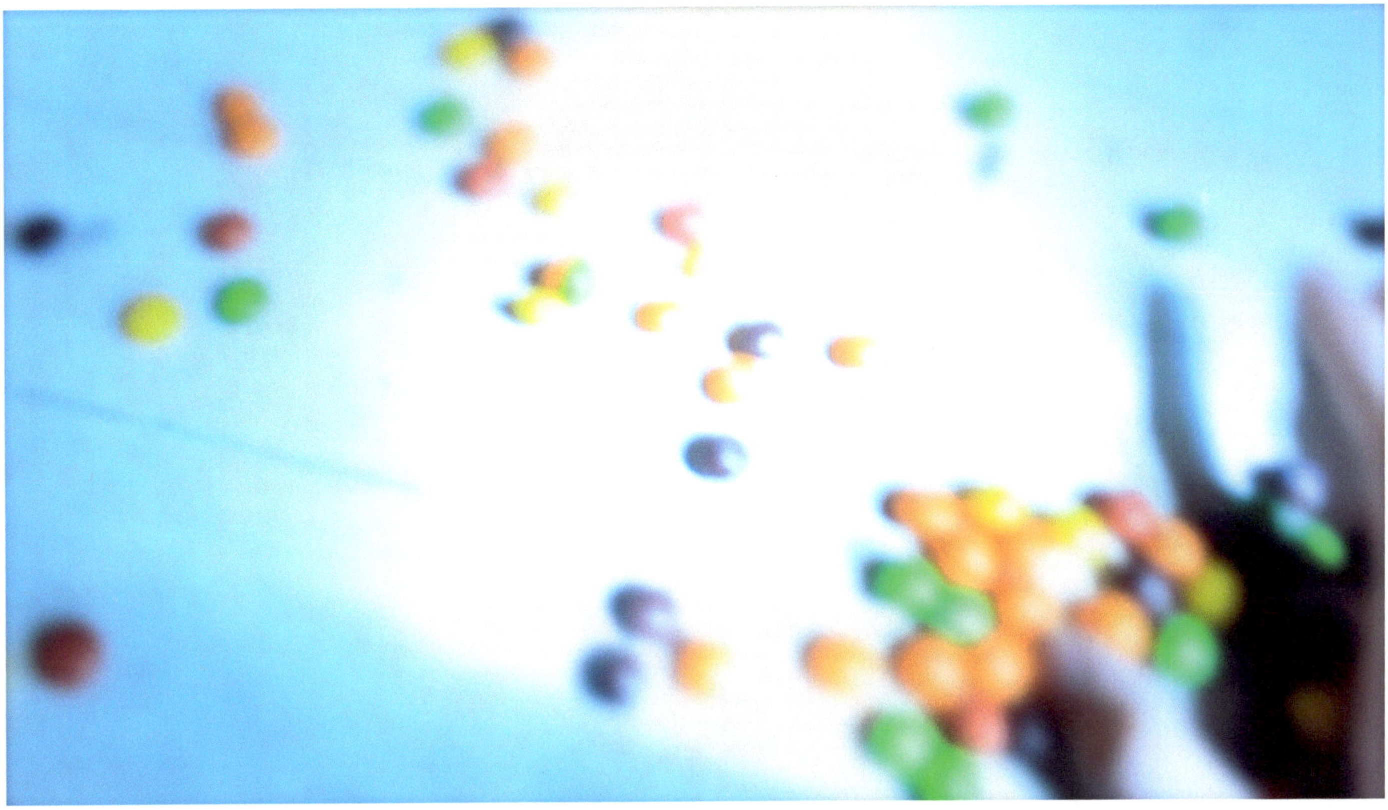

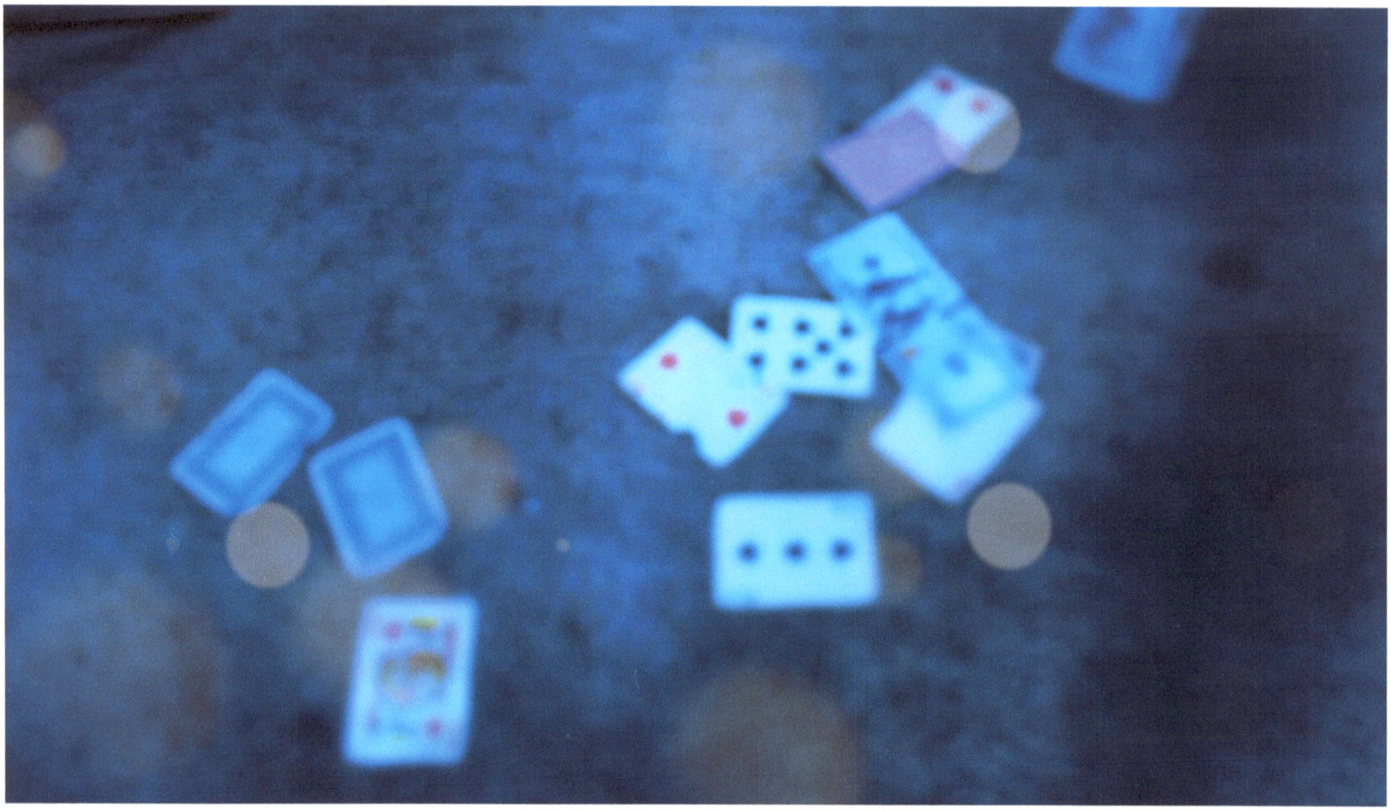

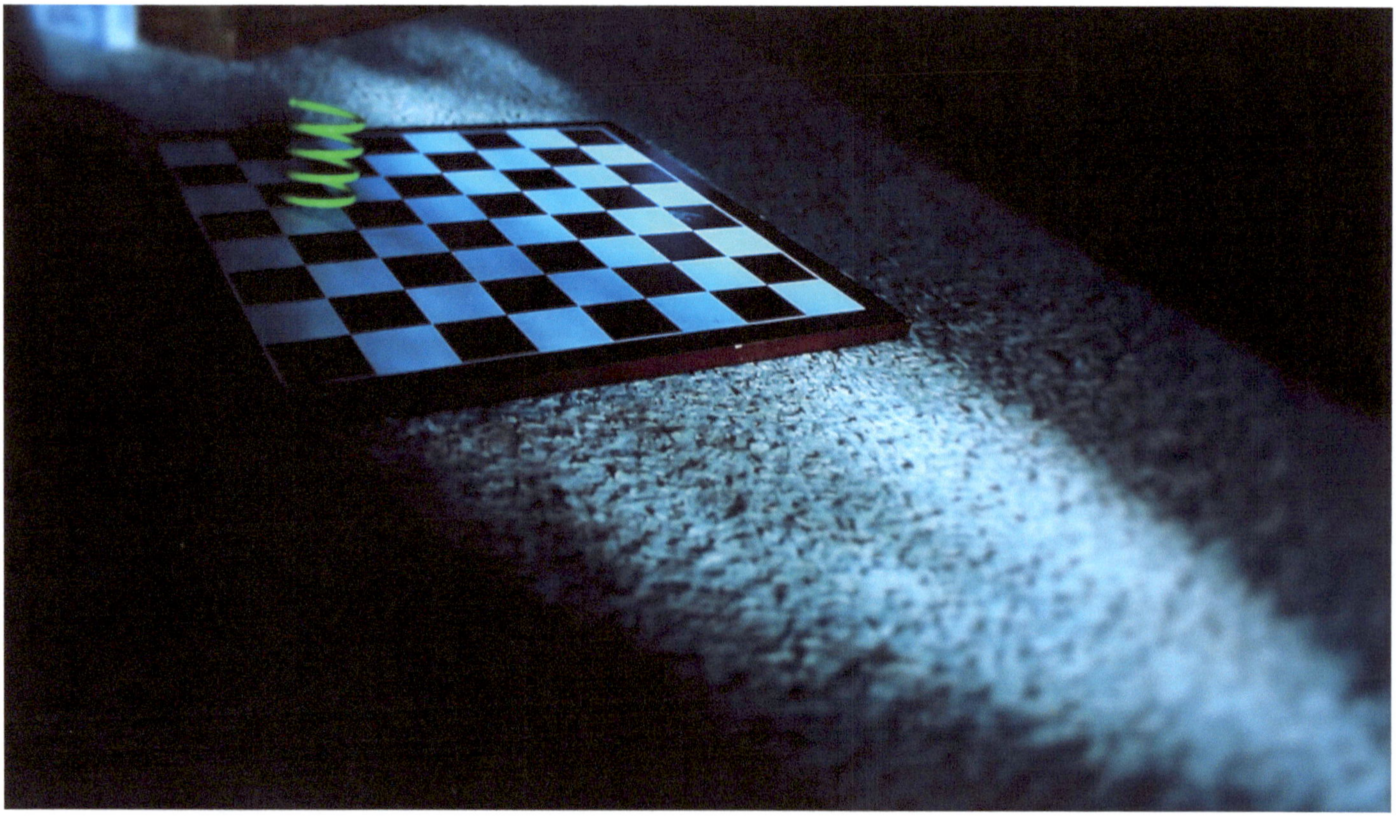

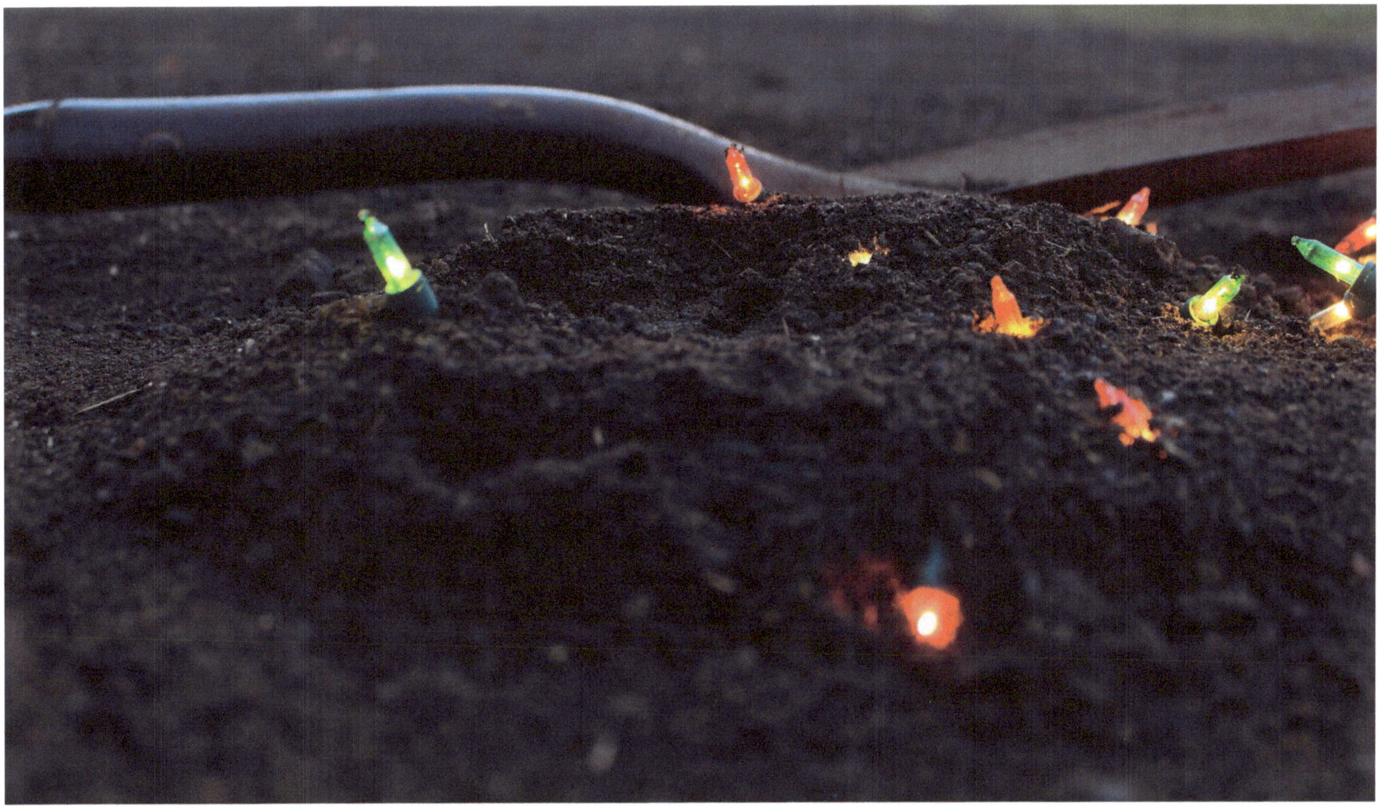

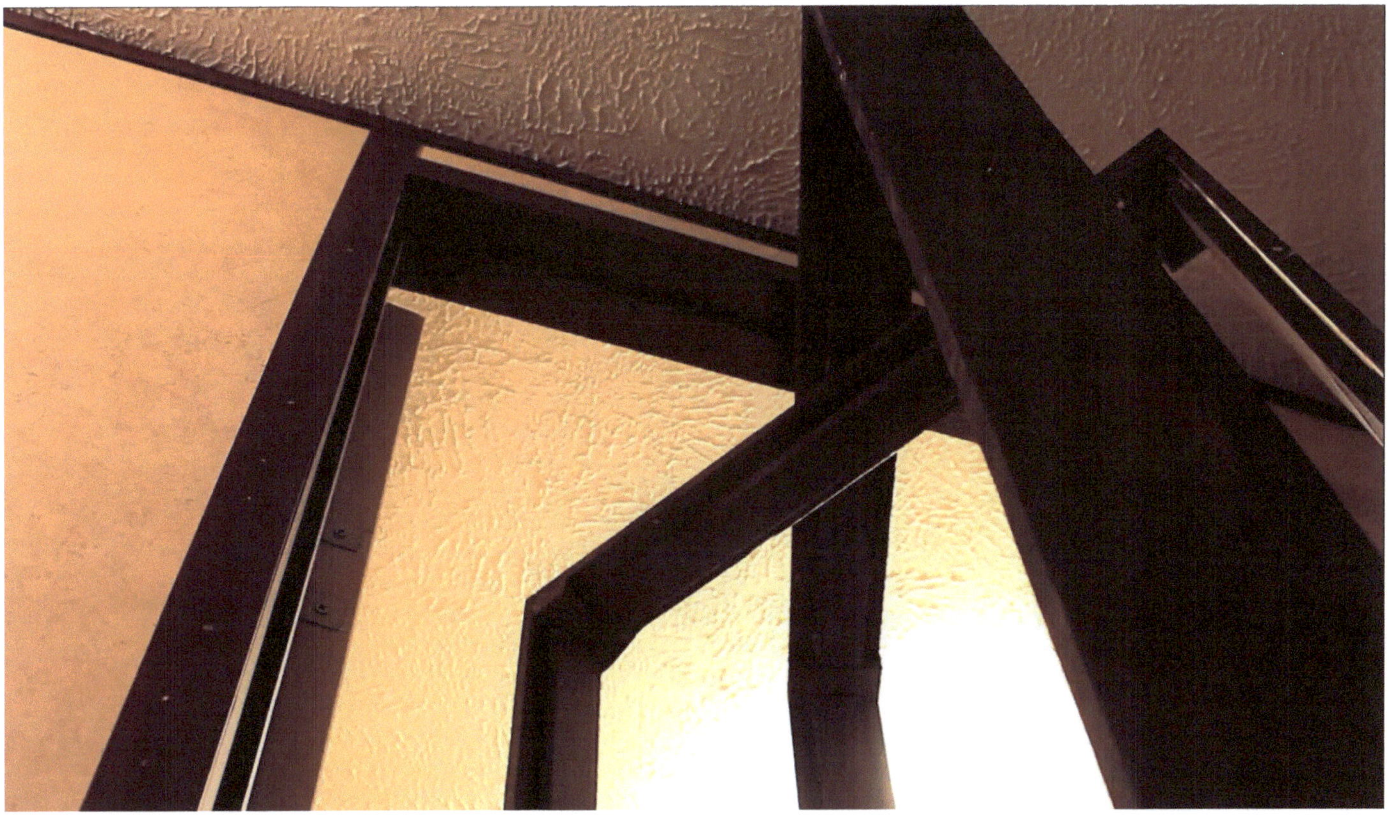

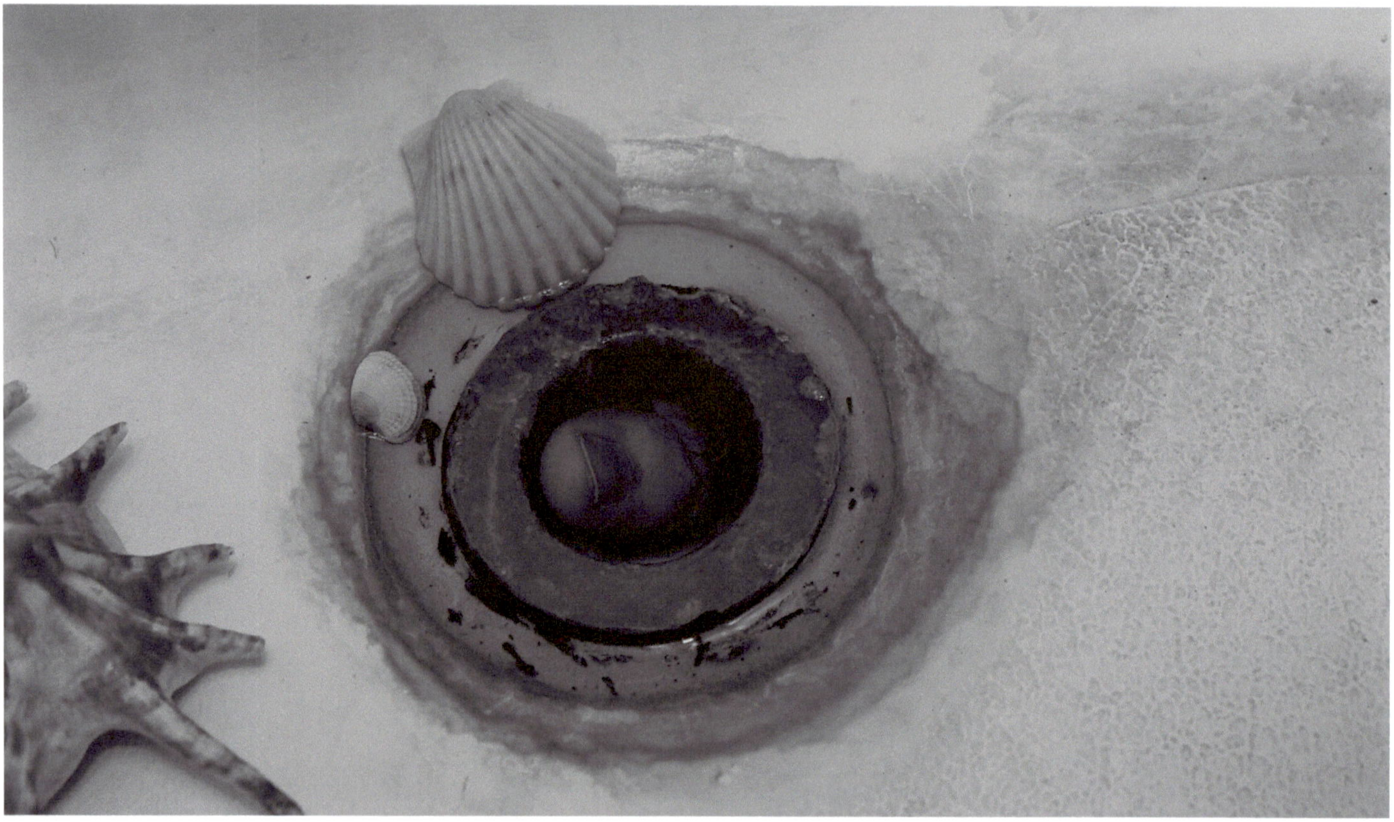

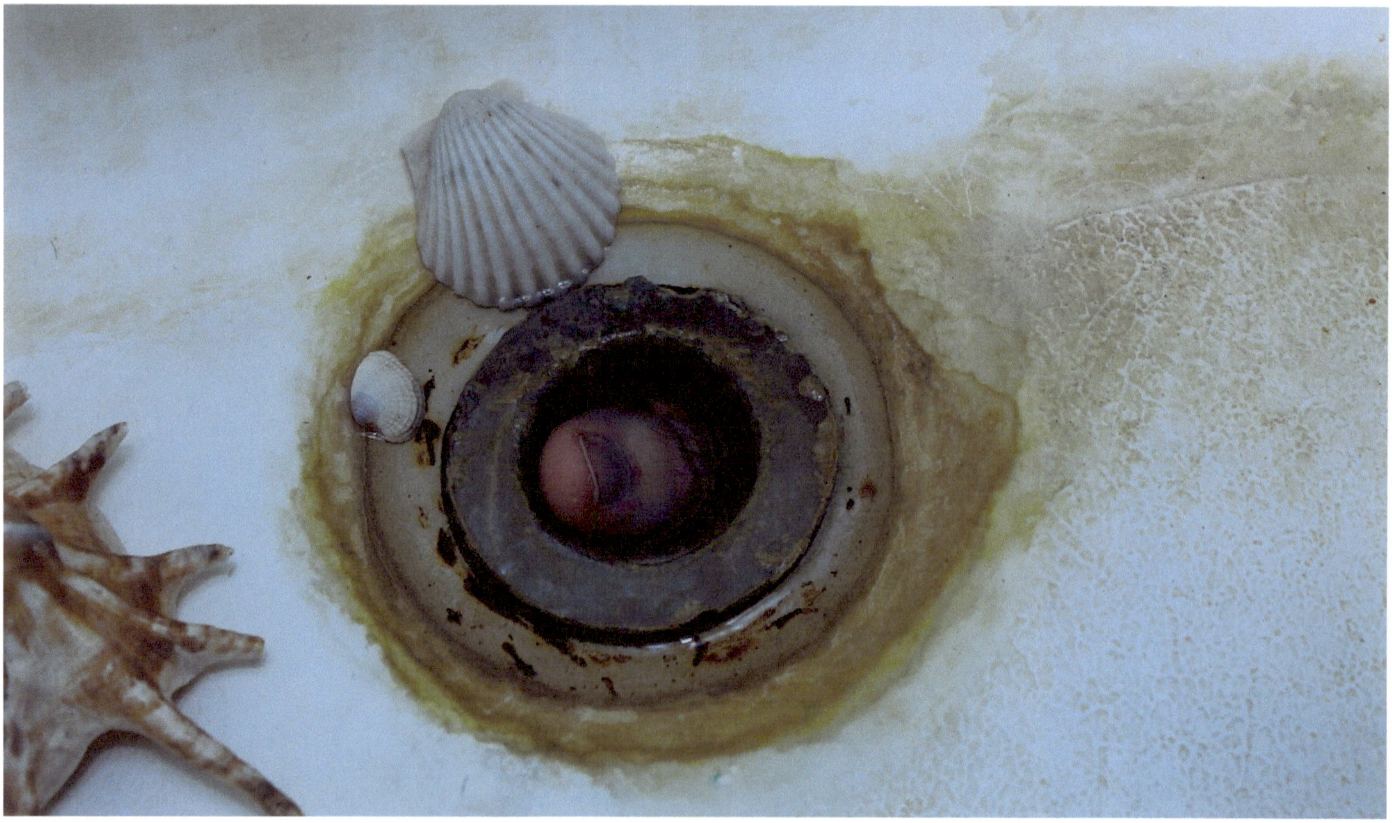

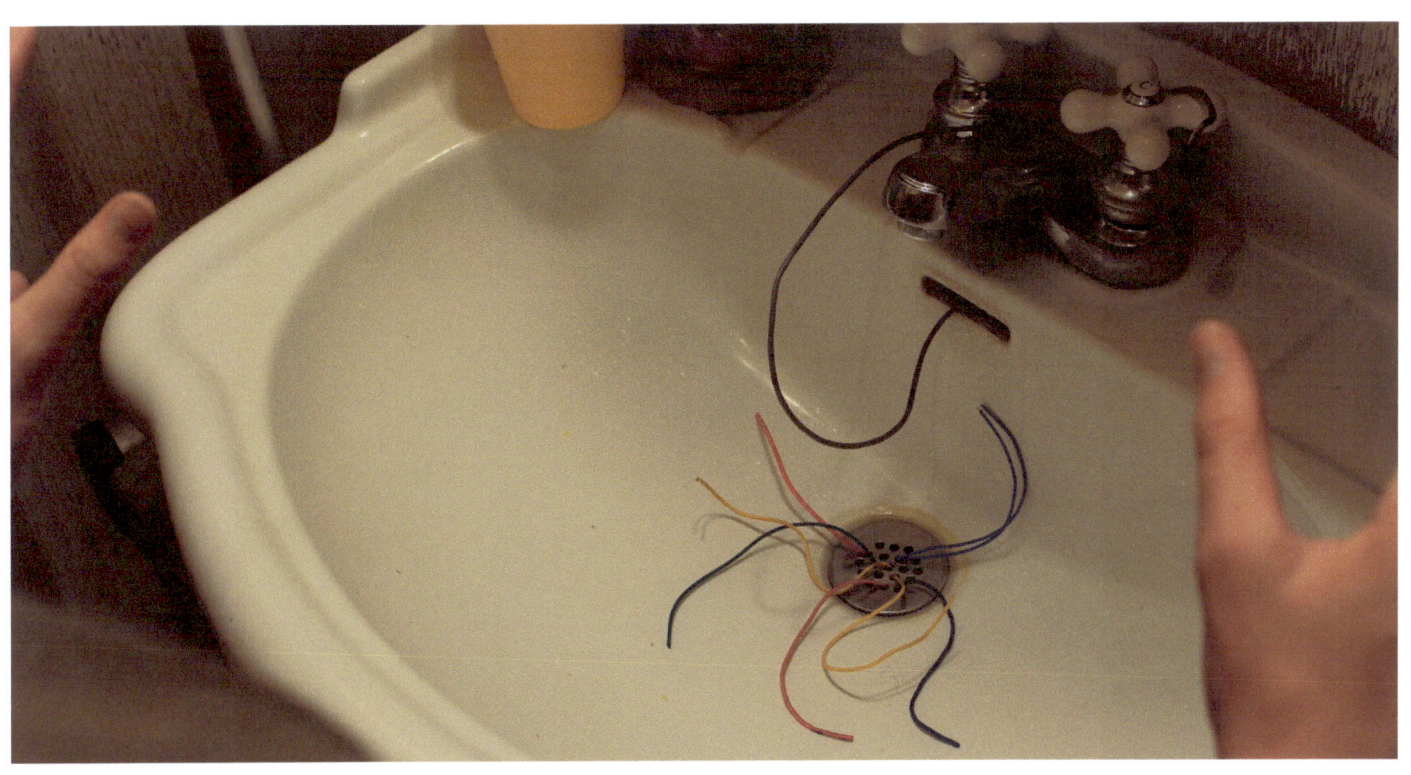

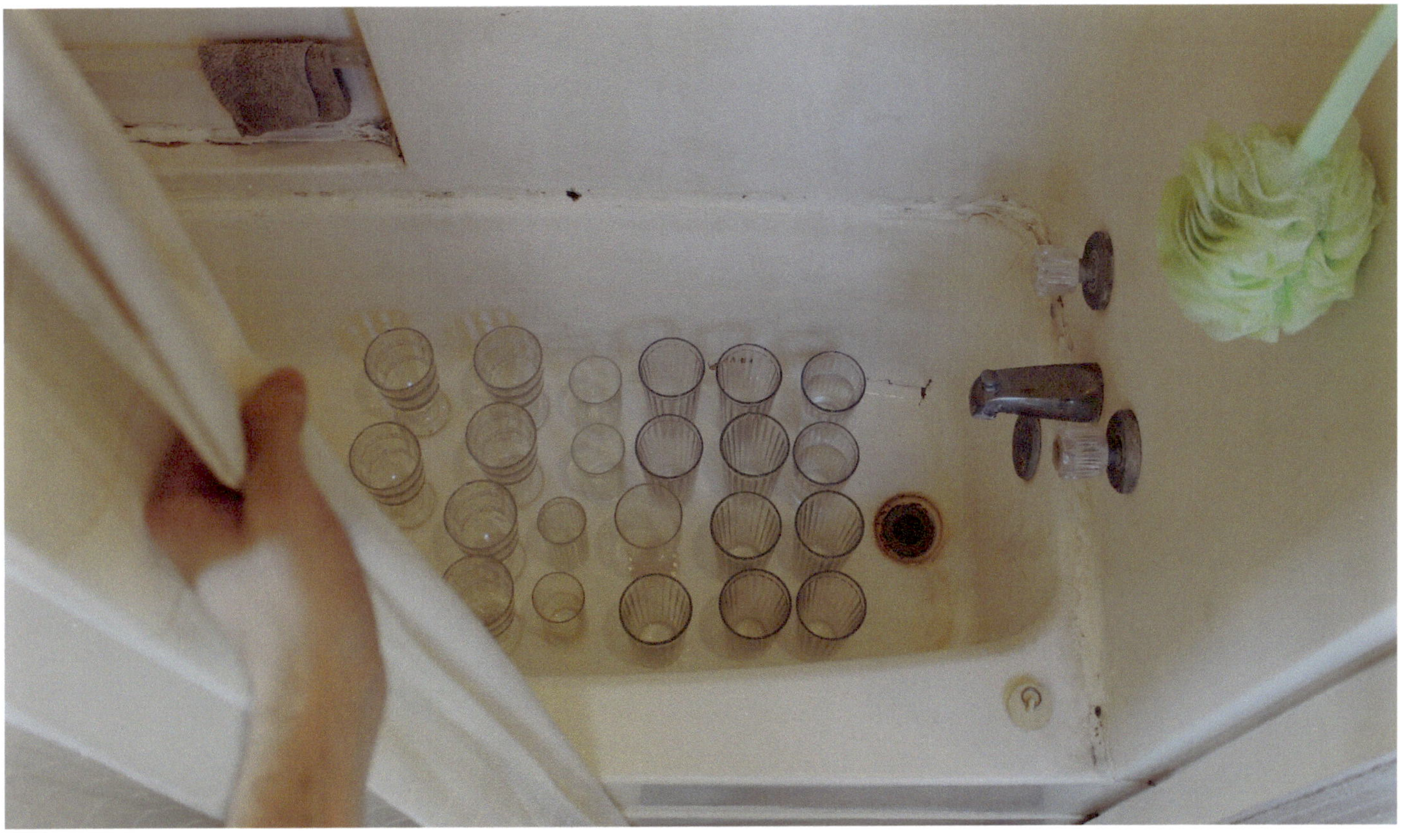

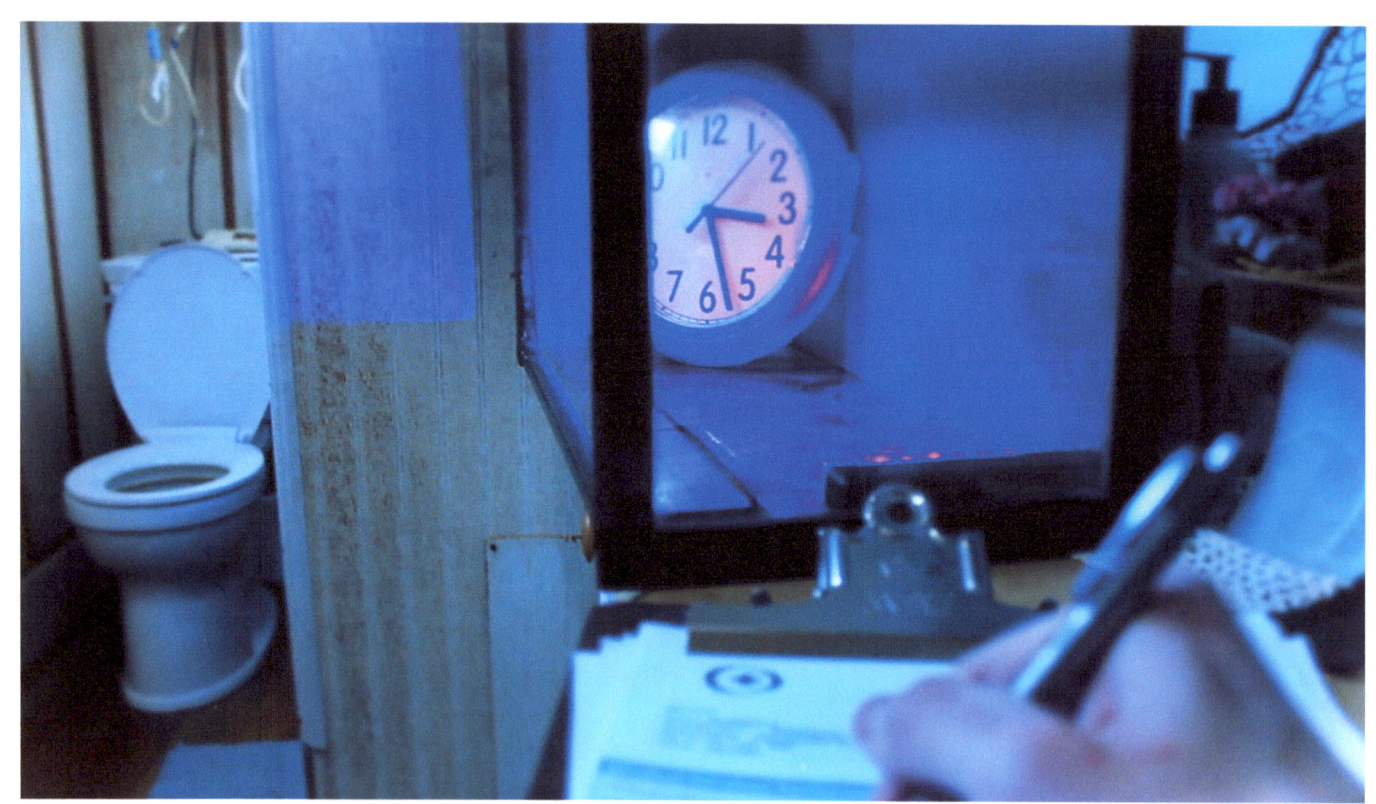

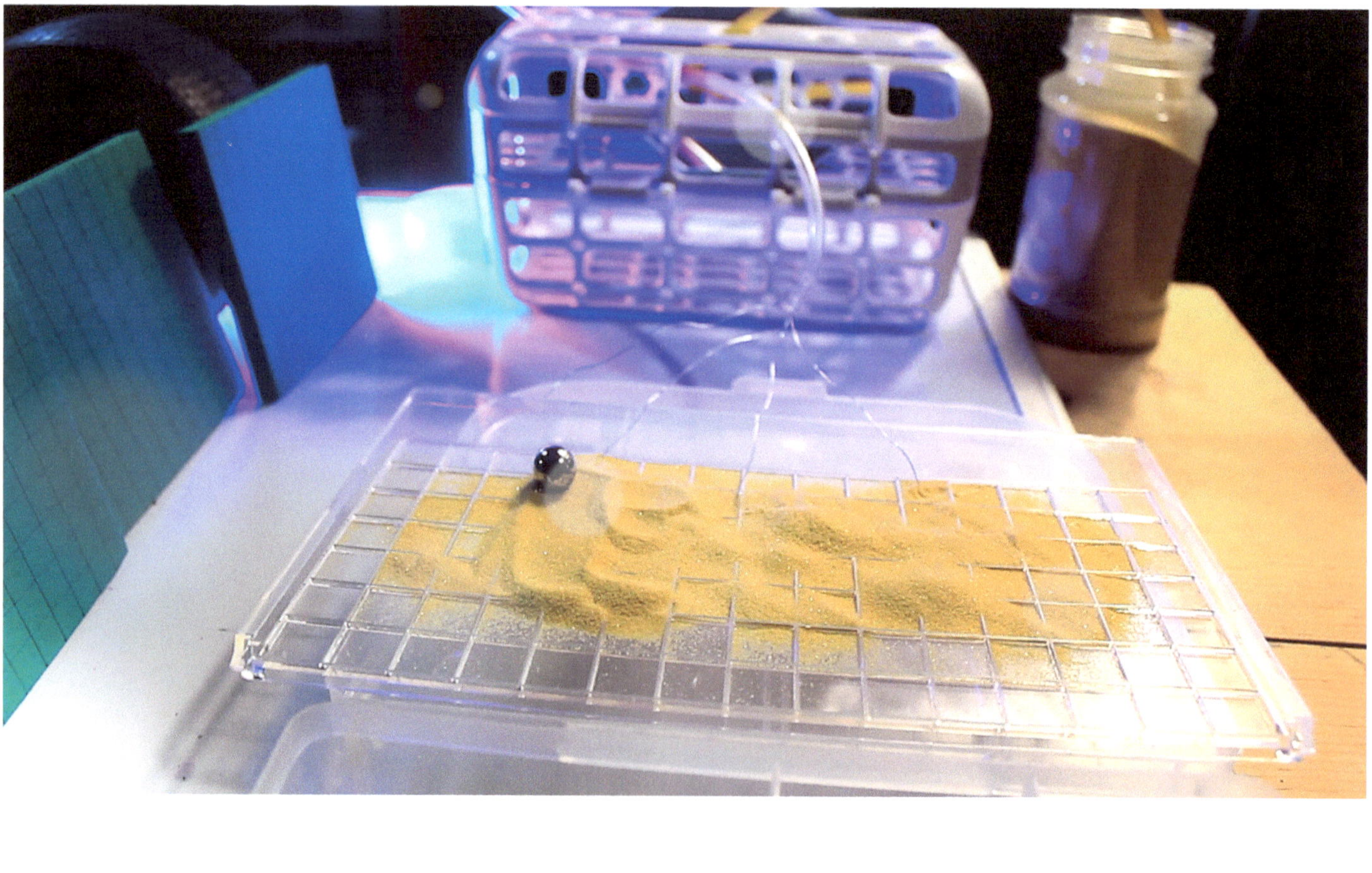

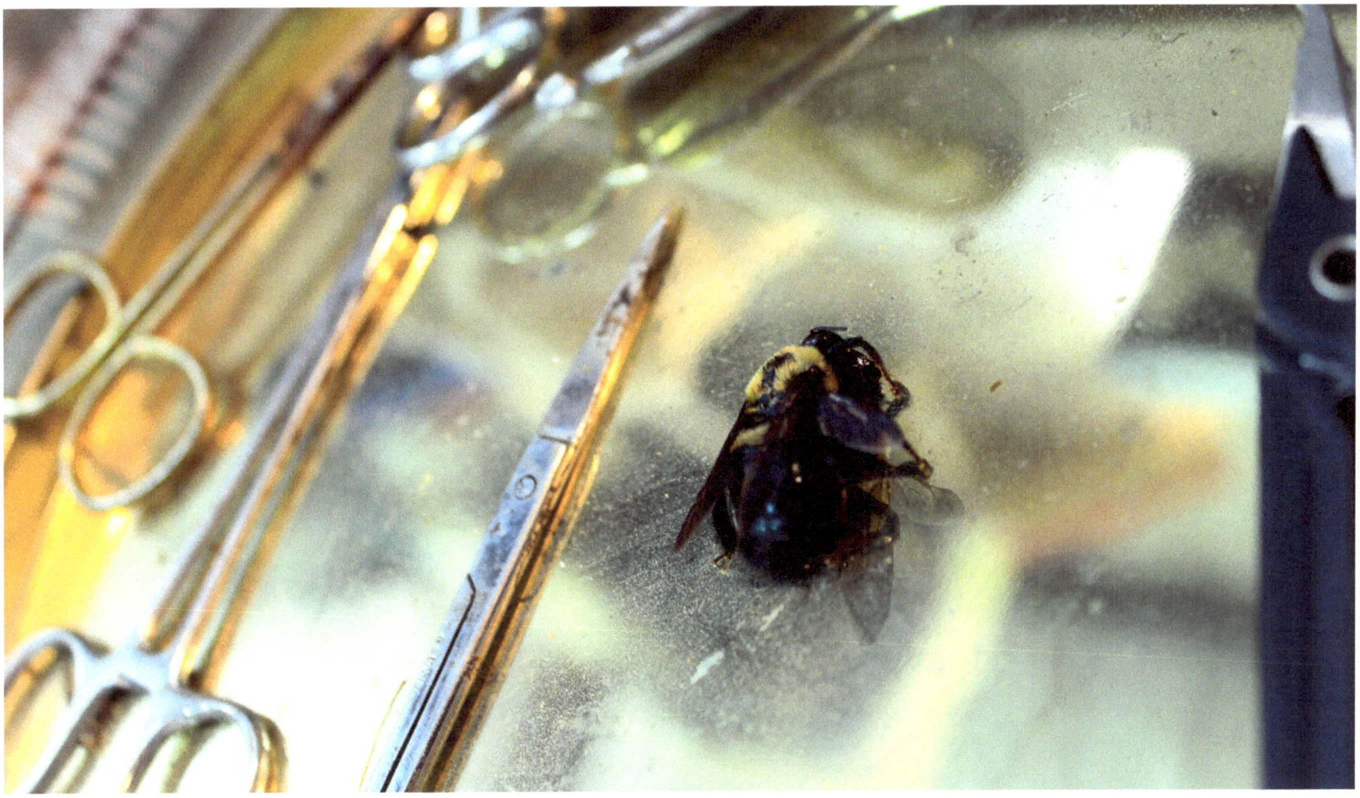

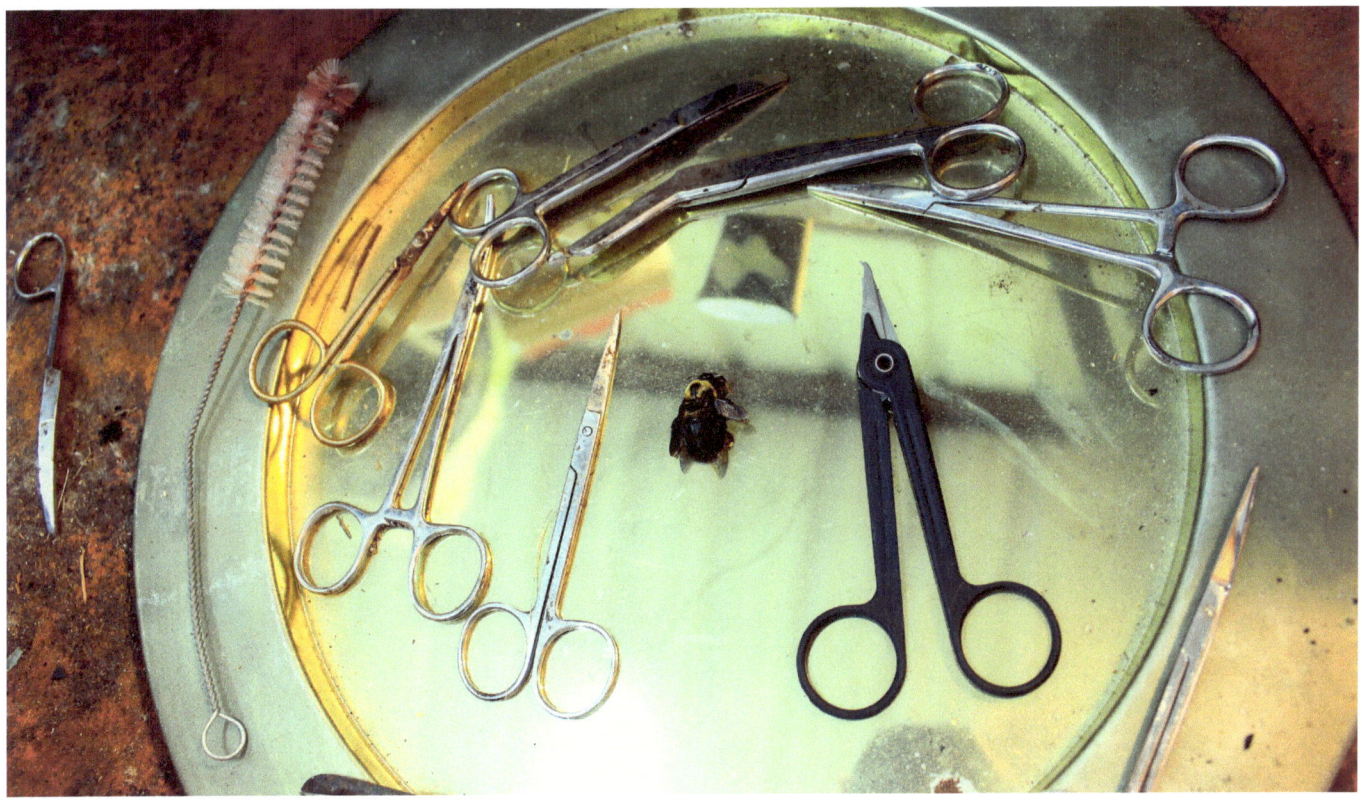

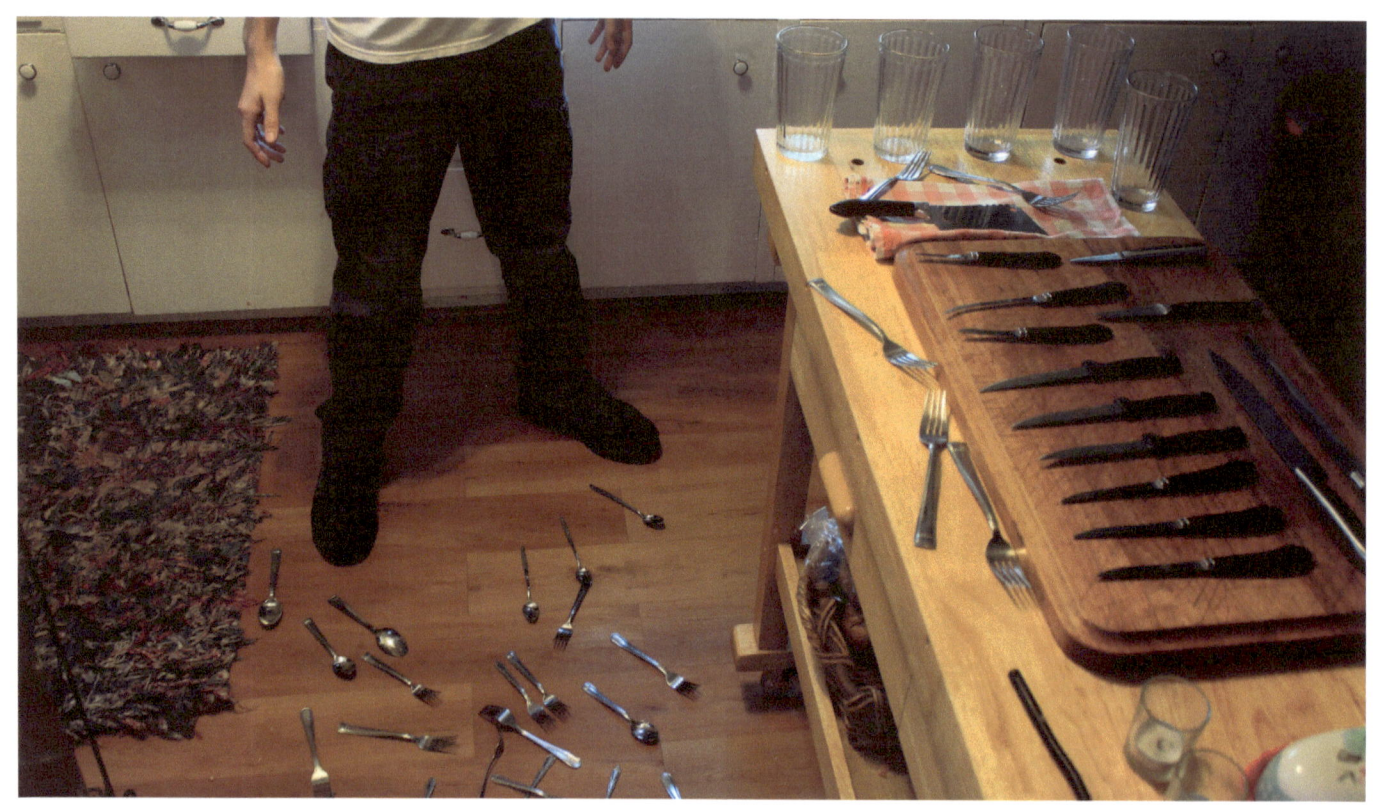

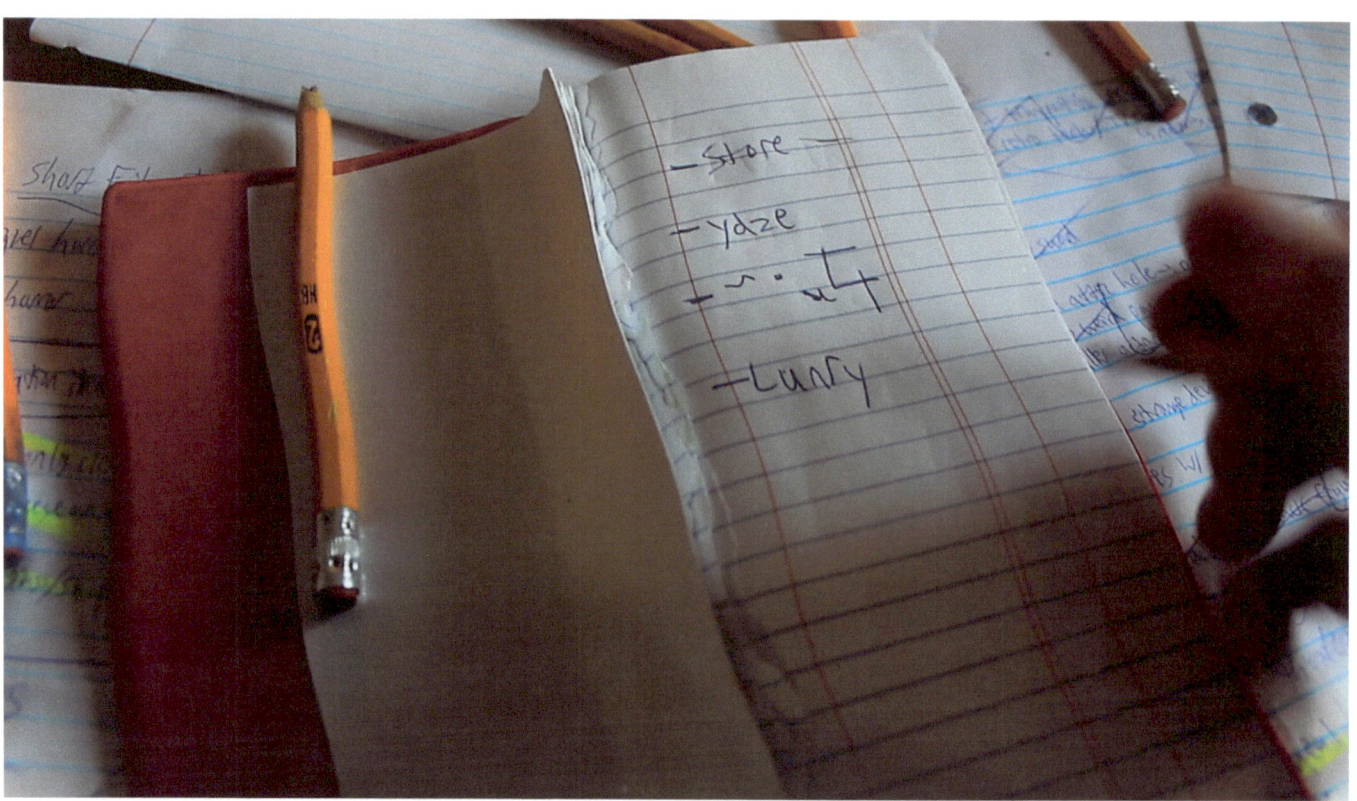

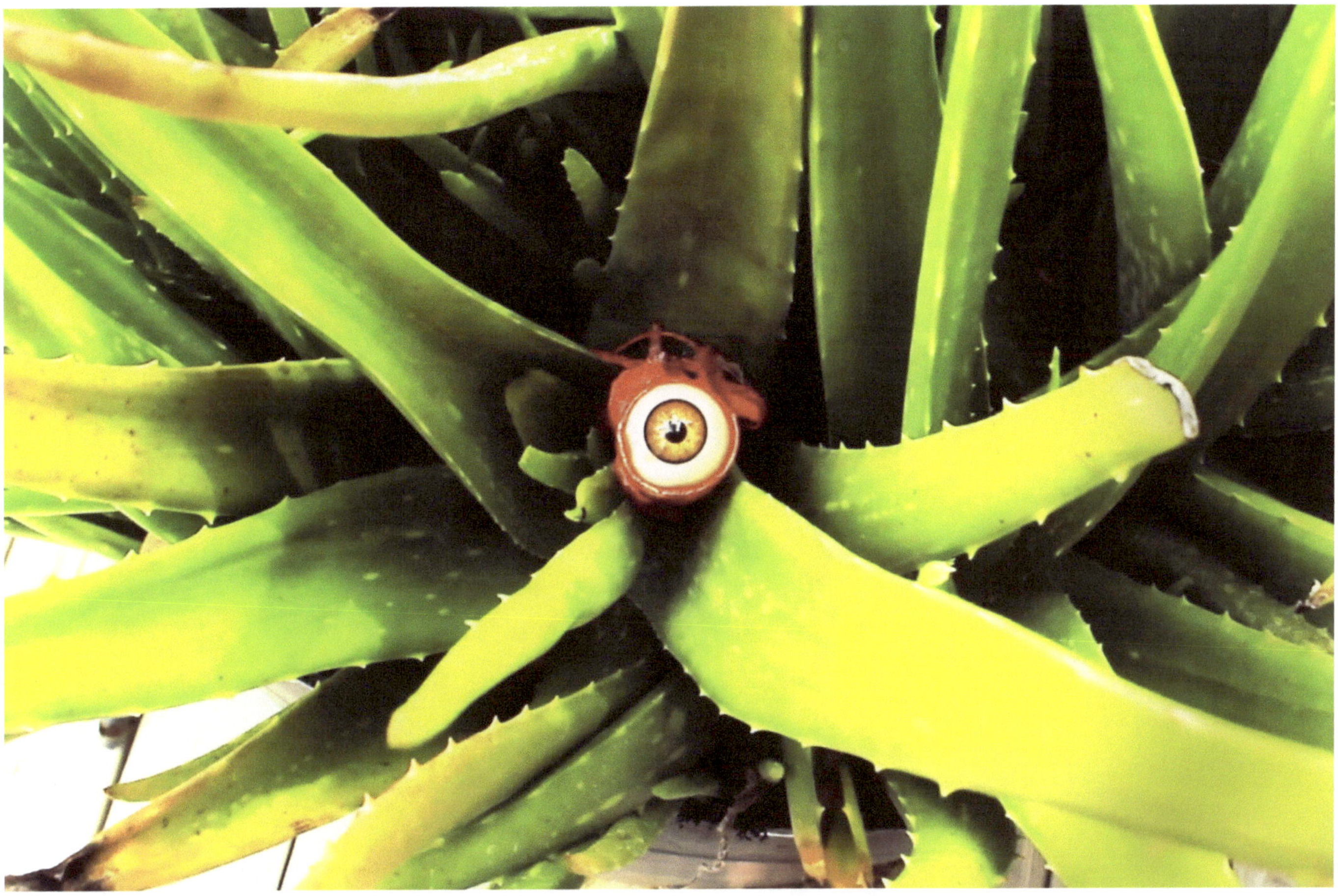

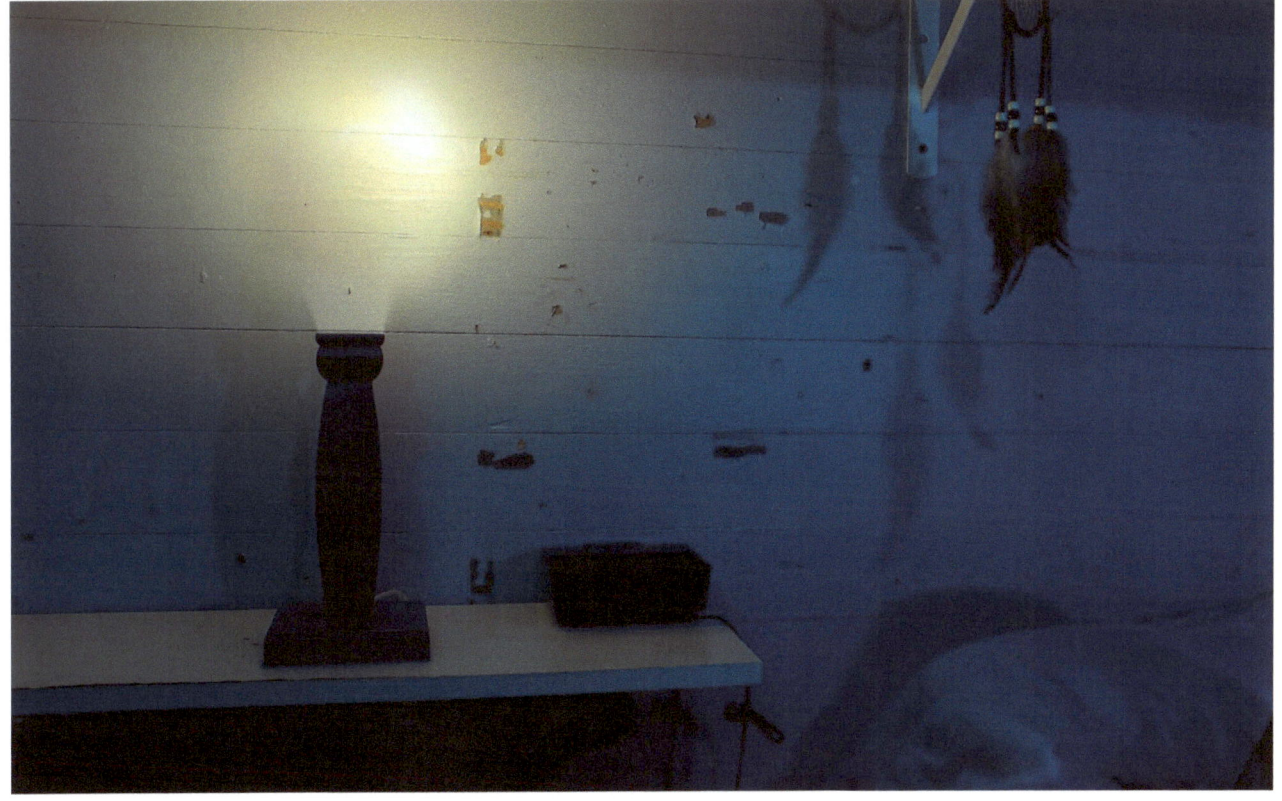

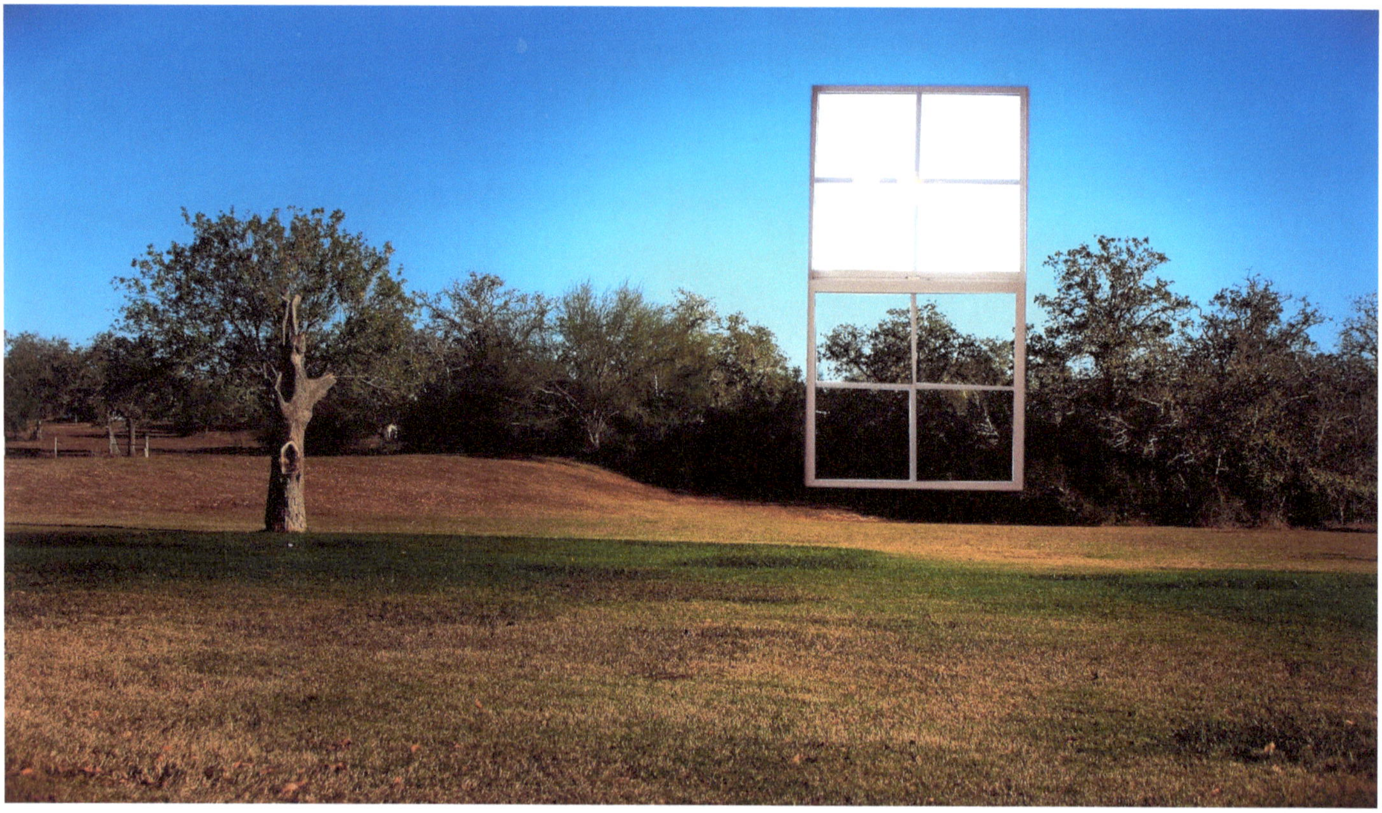

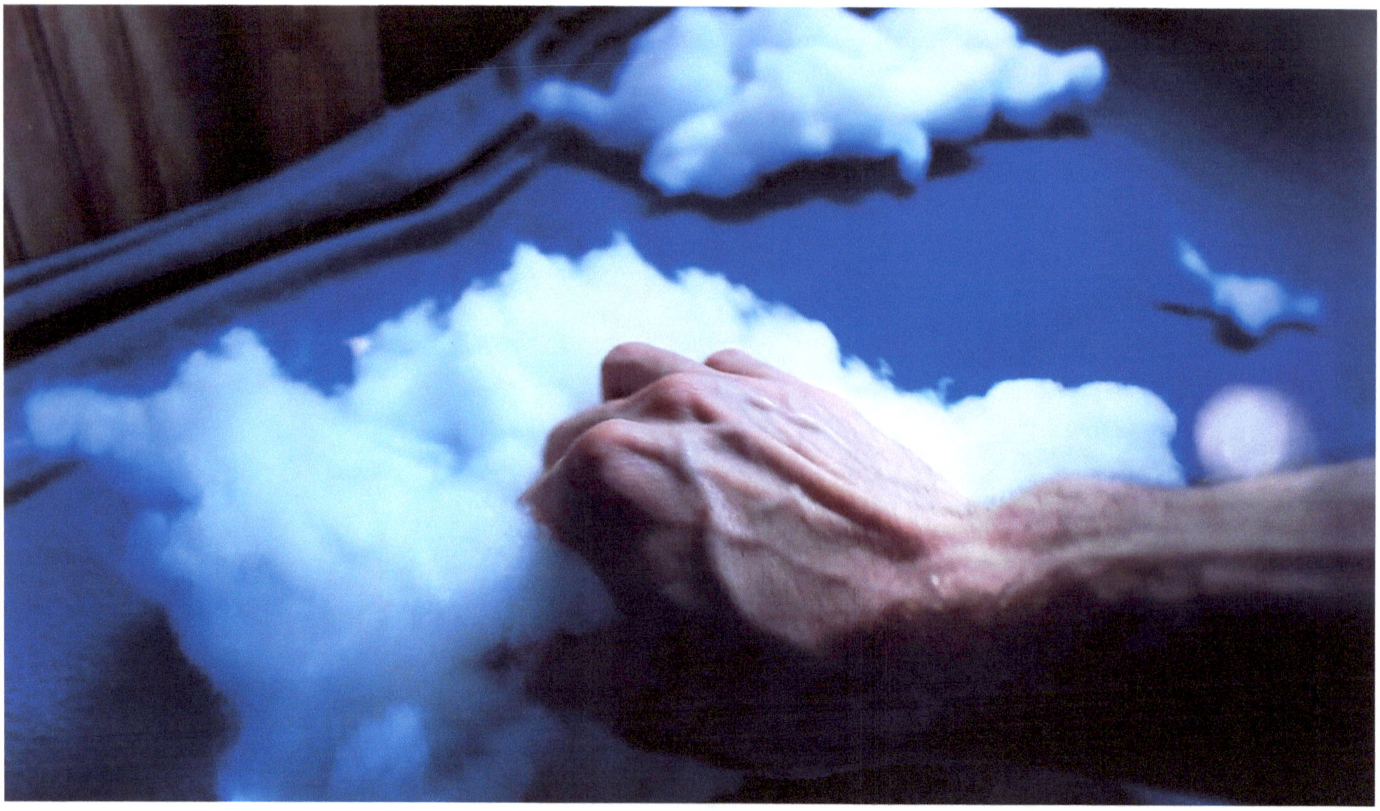

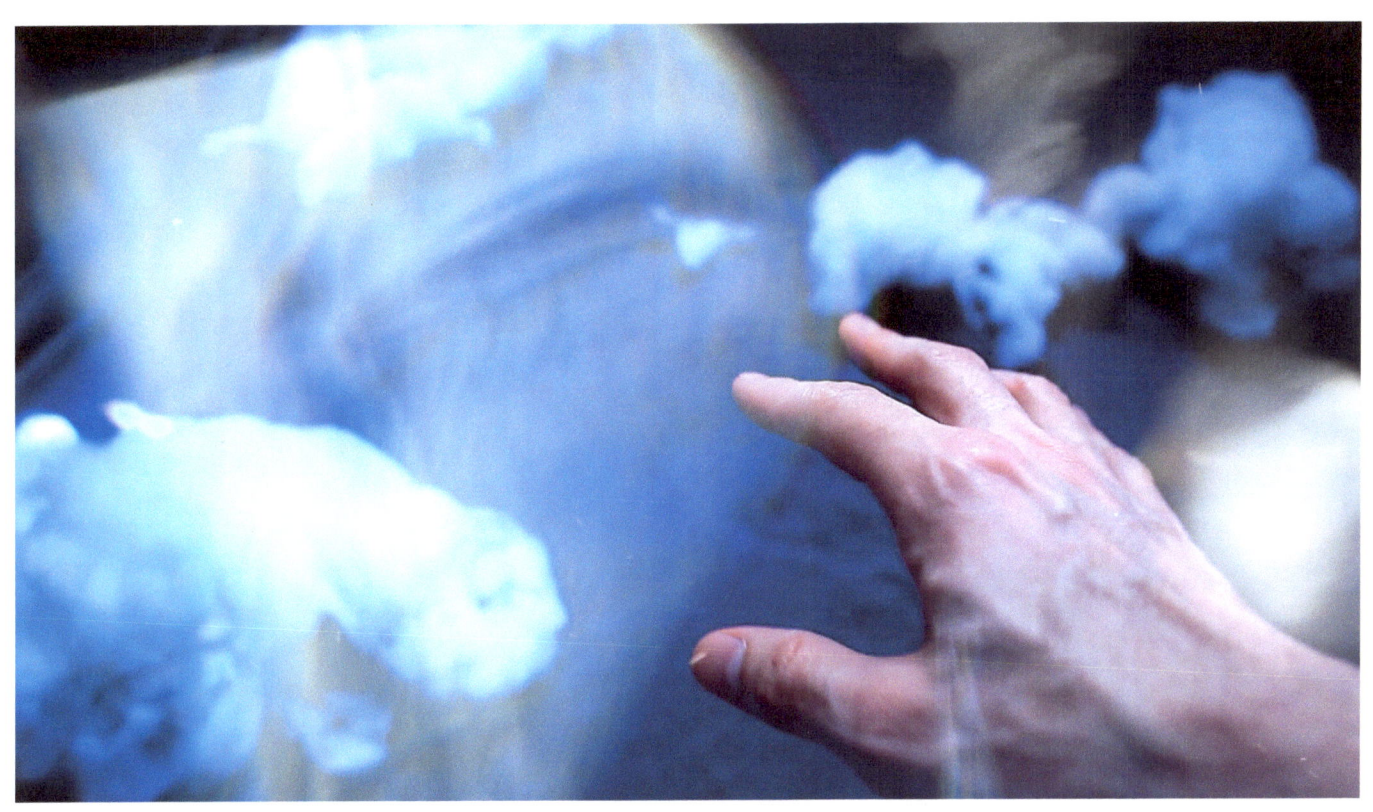

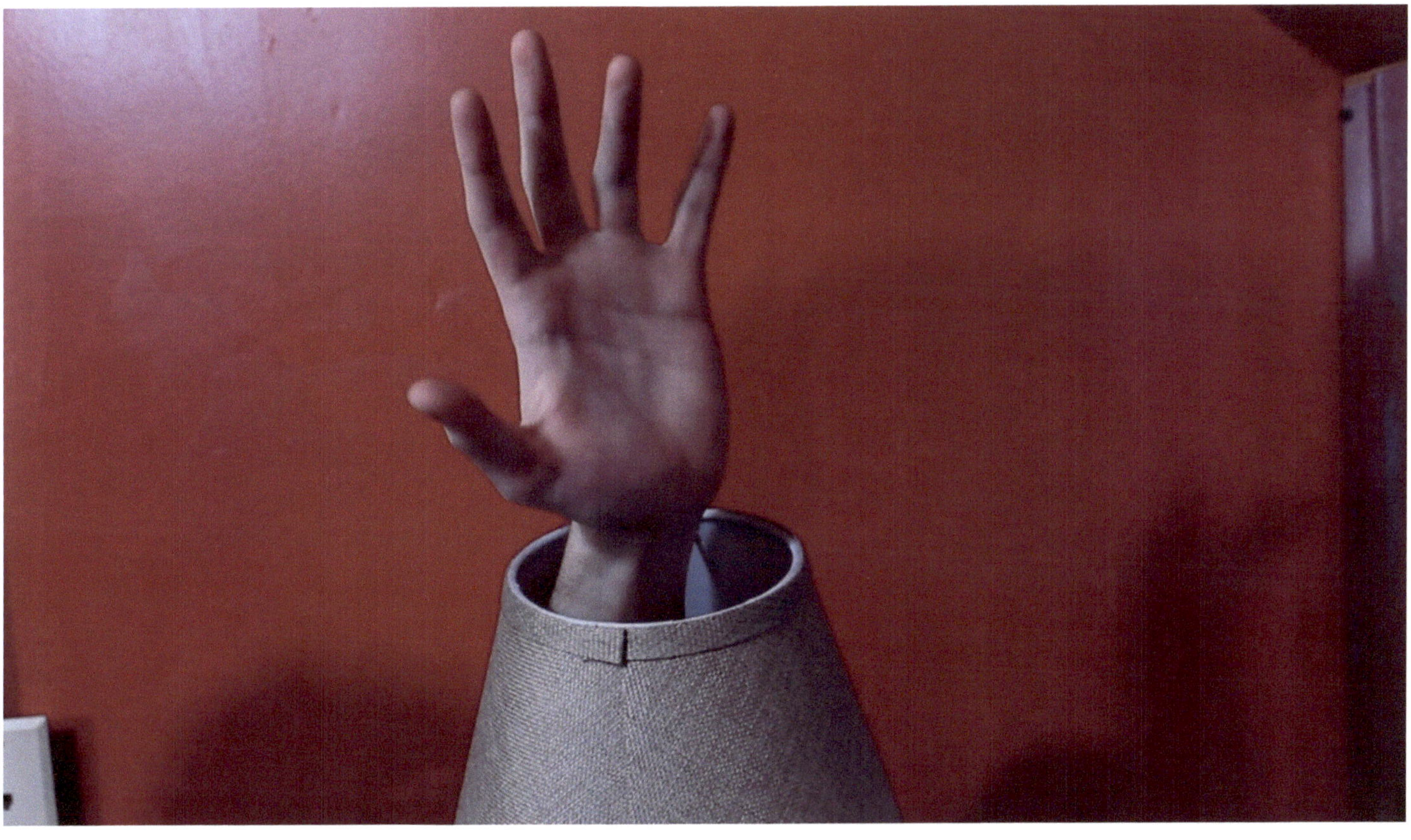

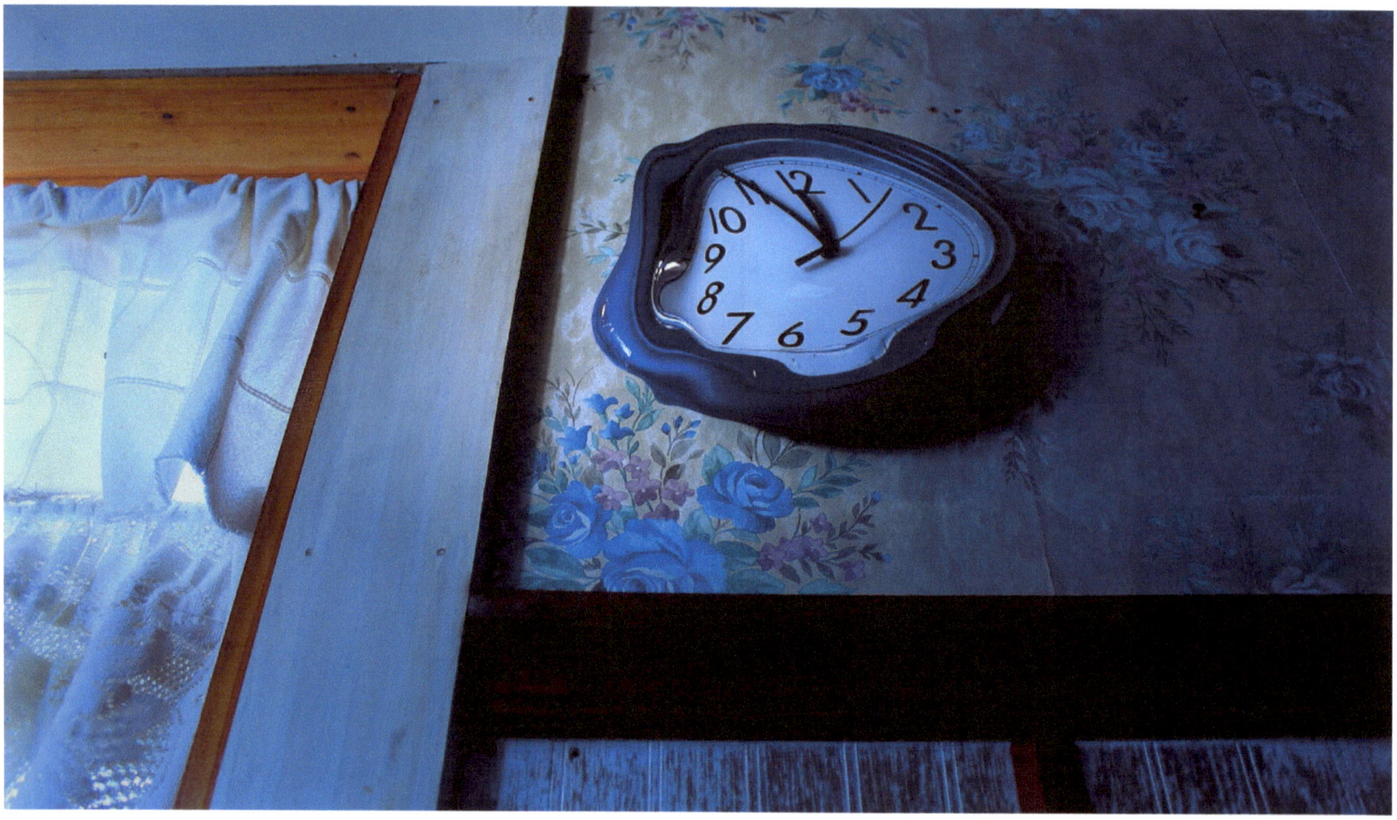

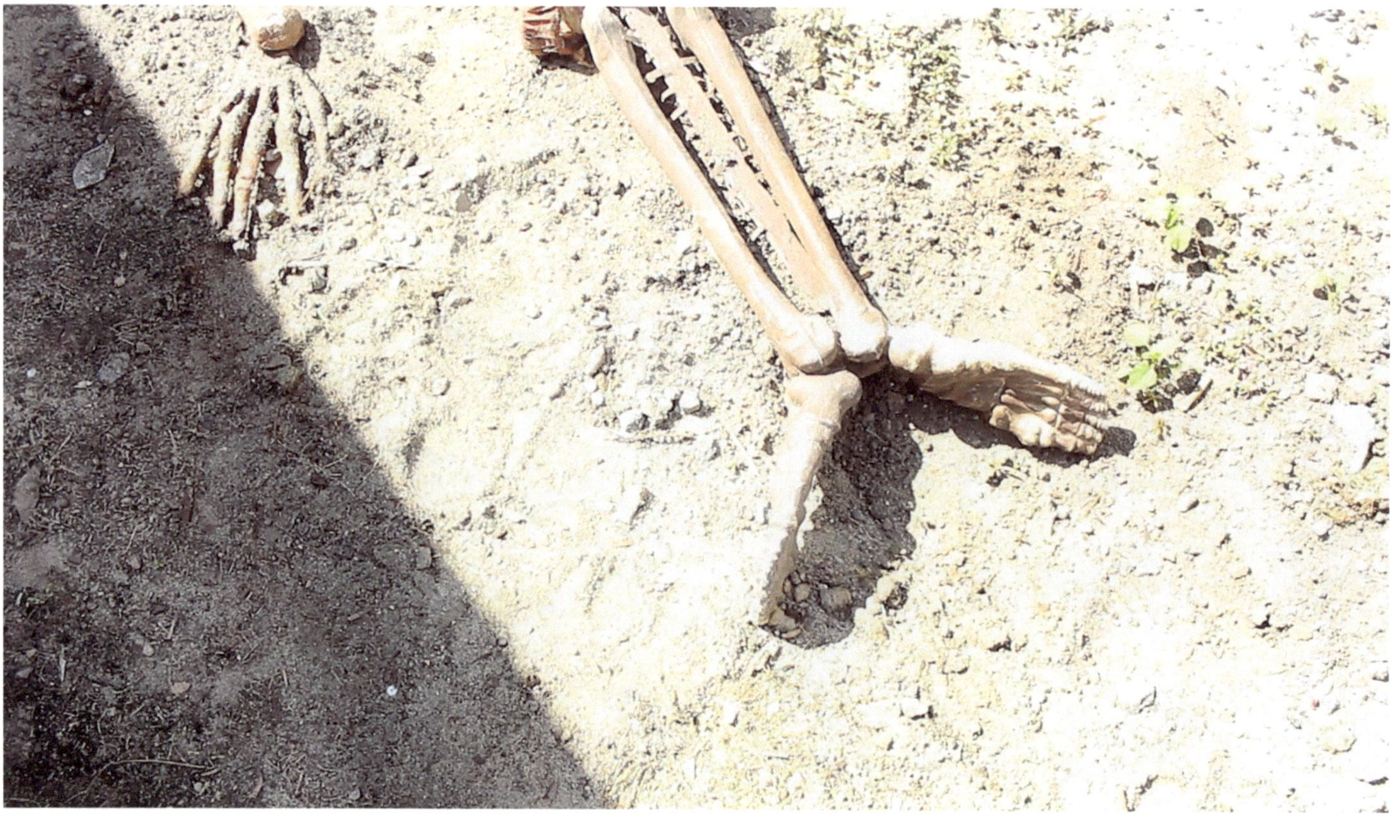

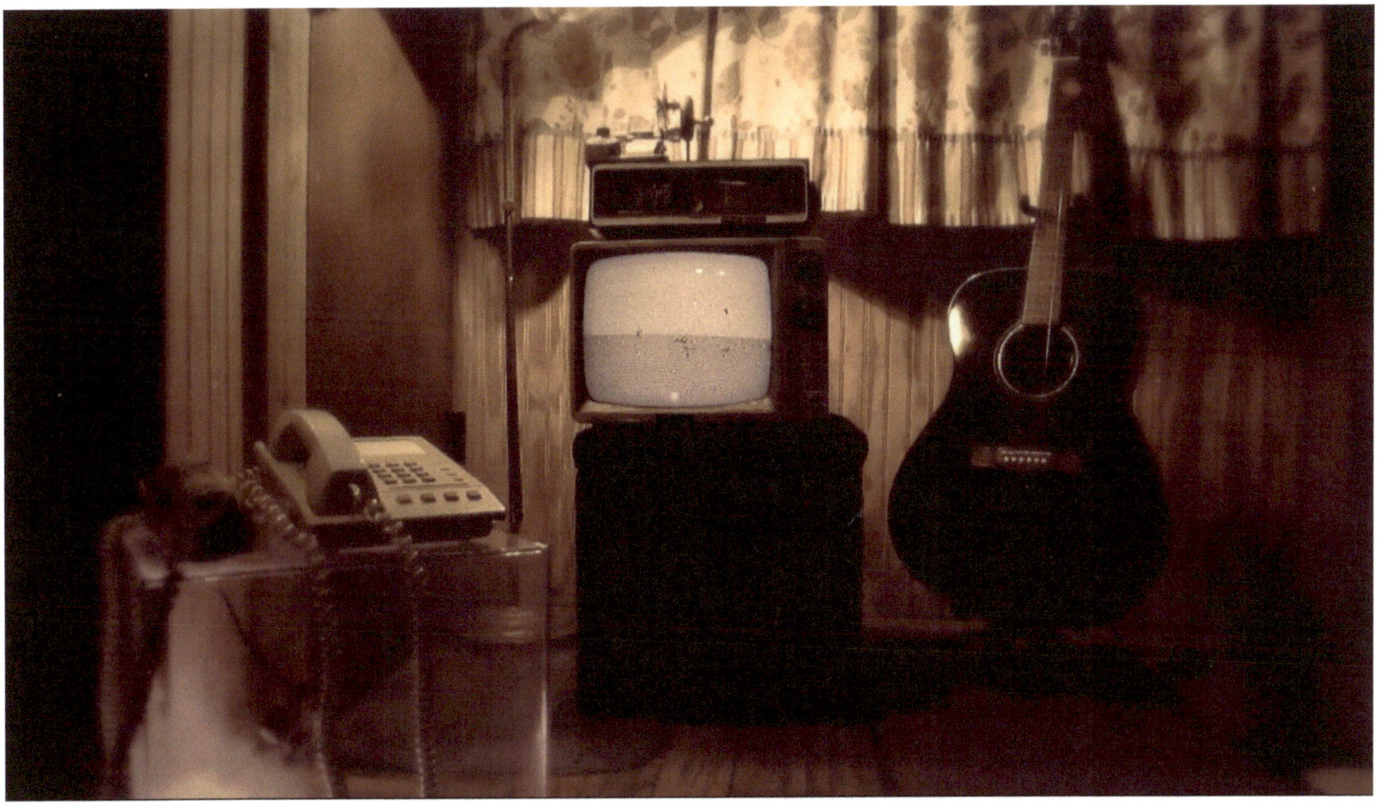

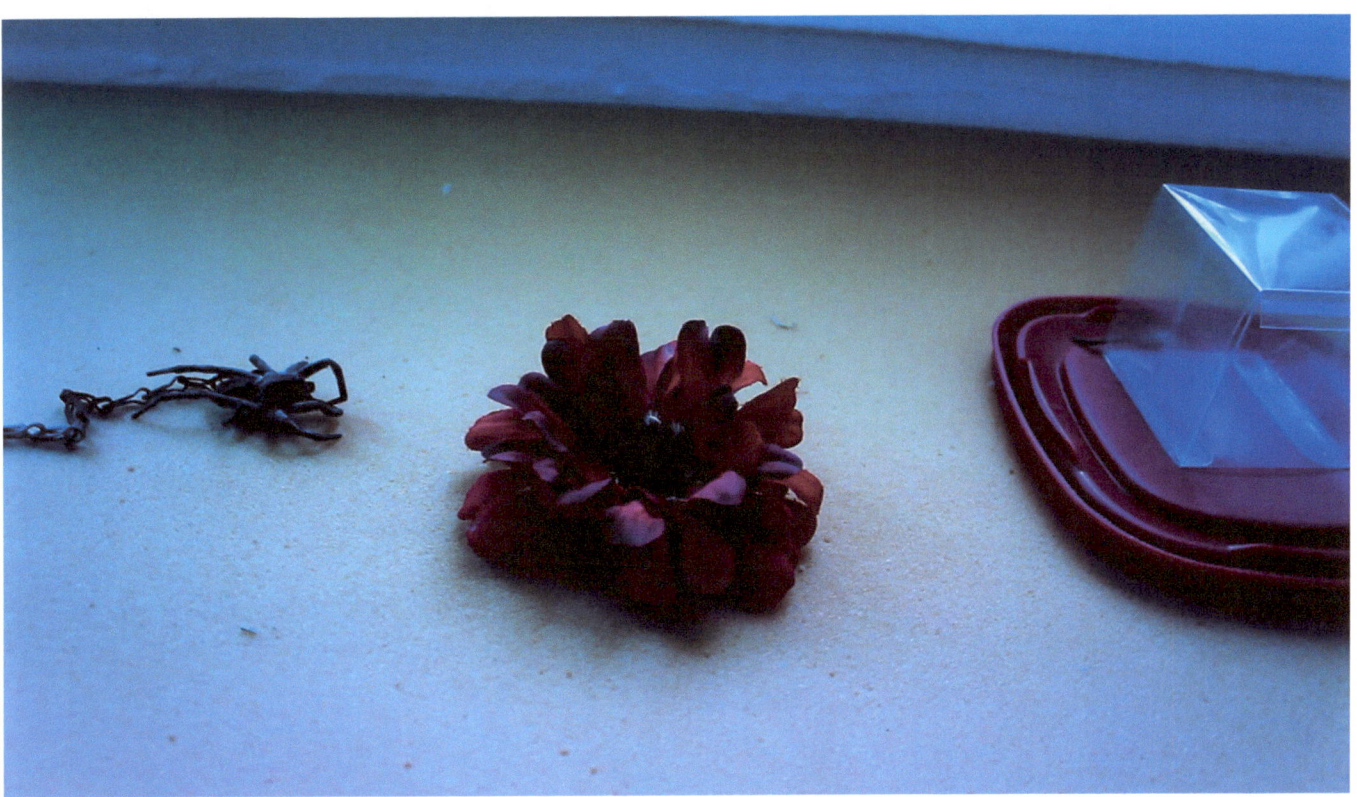

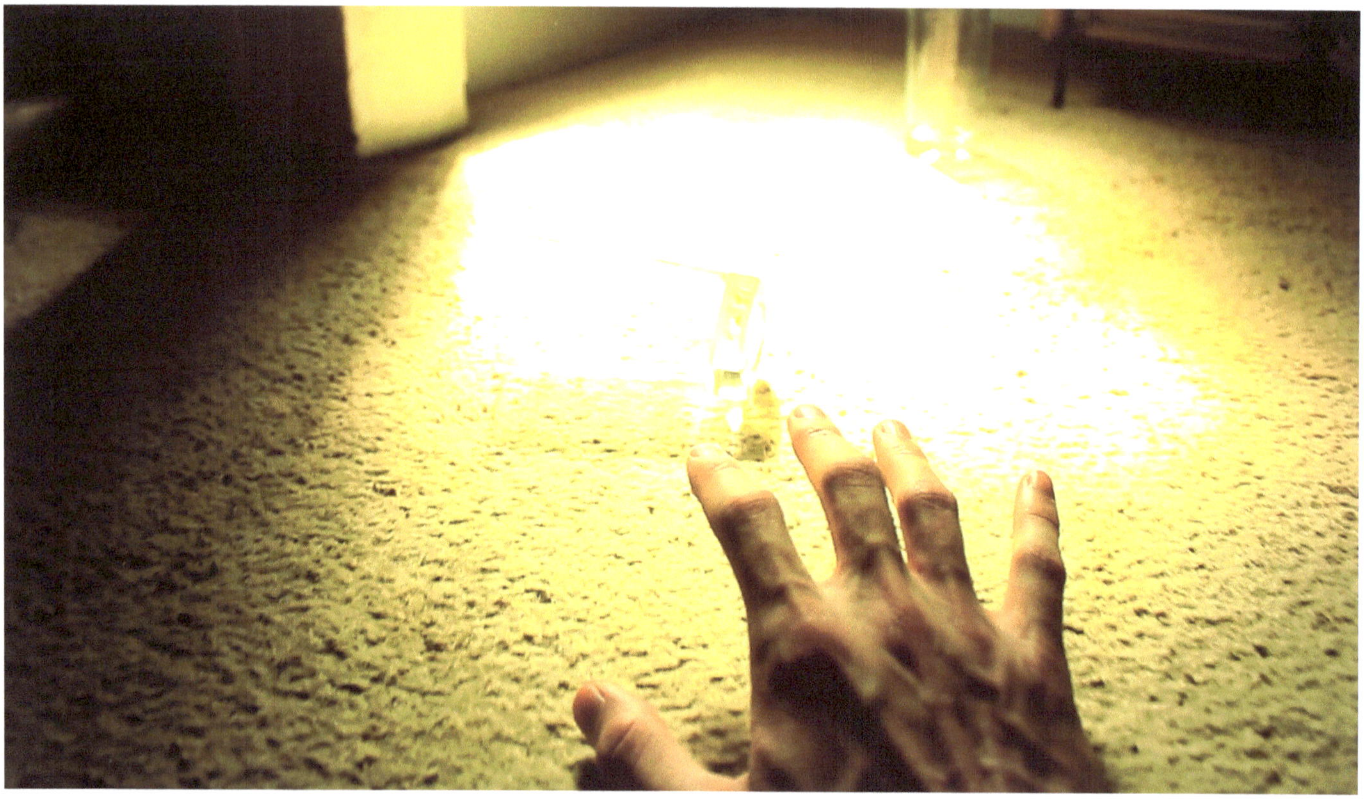

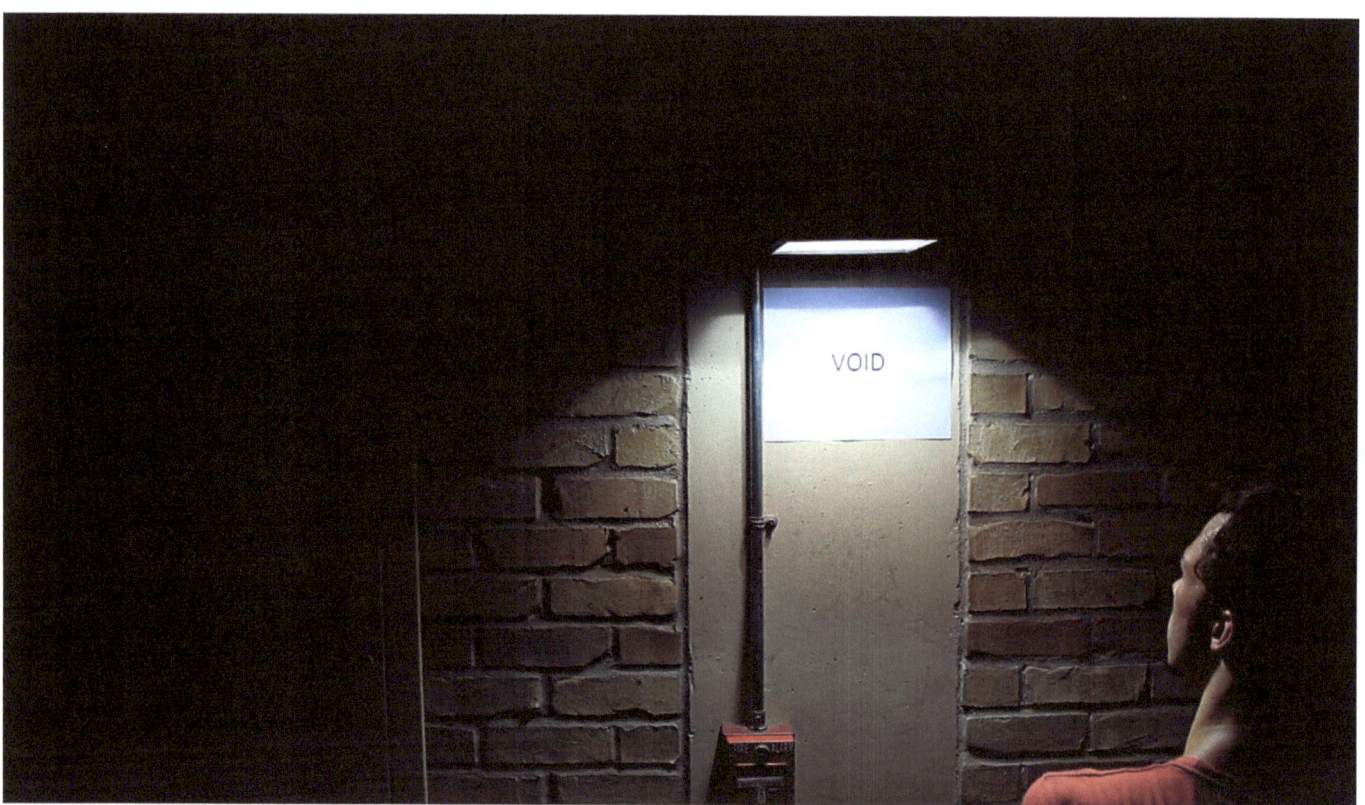

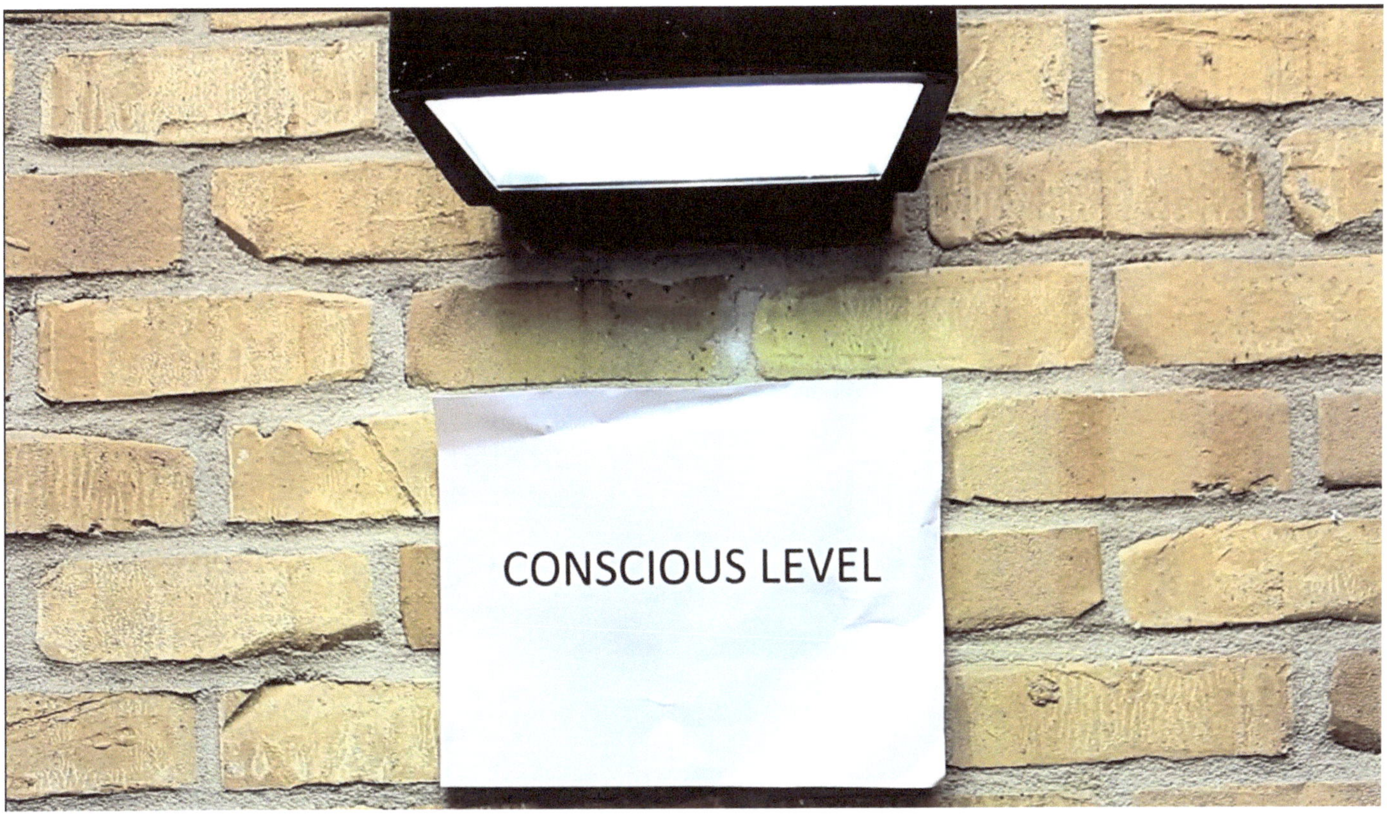

CONSCIOUS LEVEL

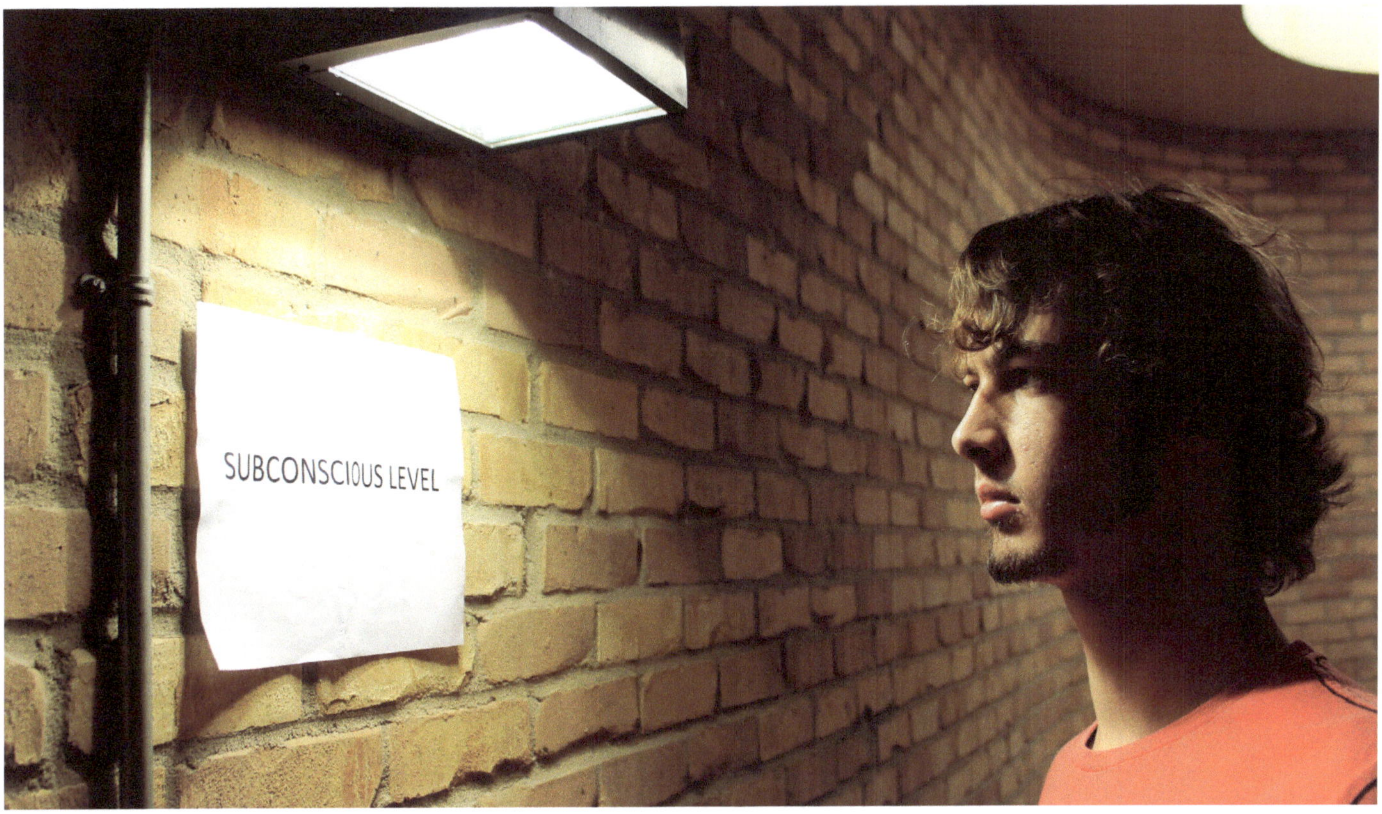

SUBCONSCIOUS LEVEL

Nightmares.

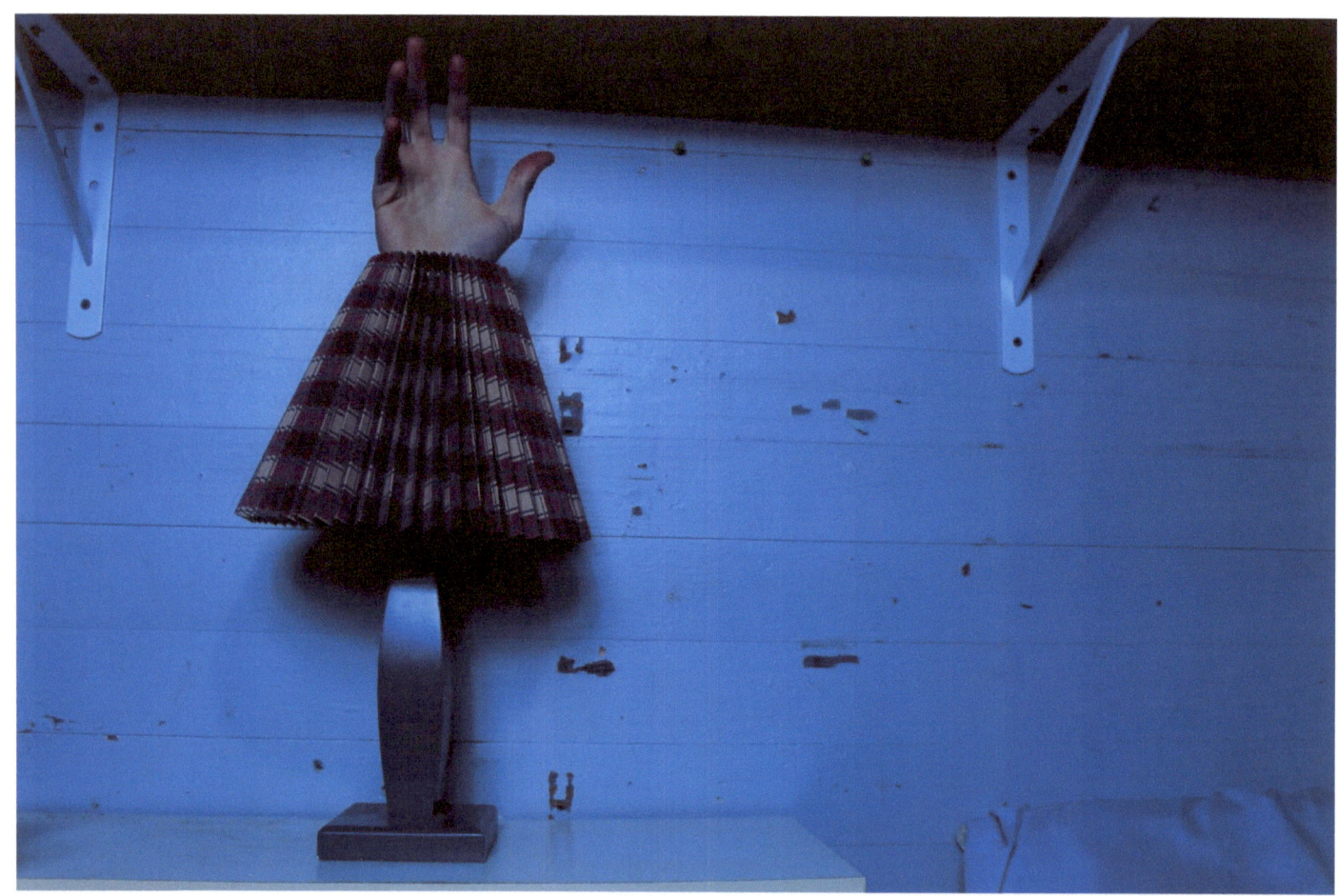

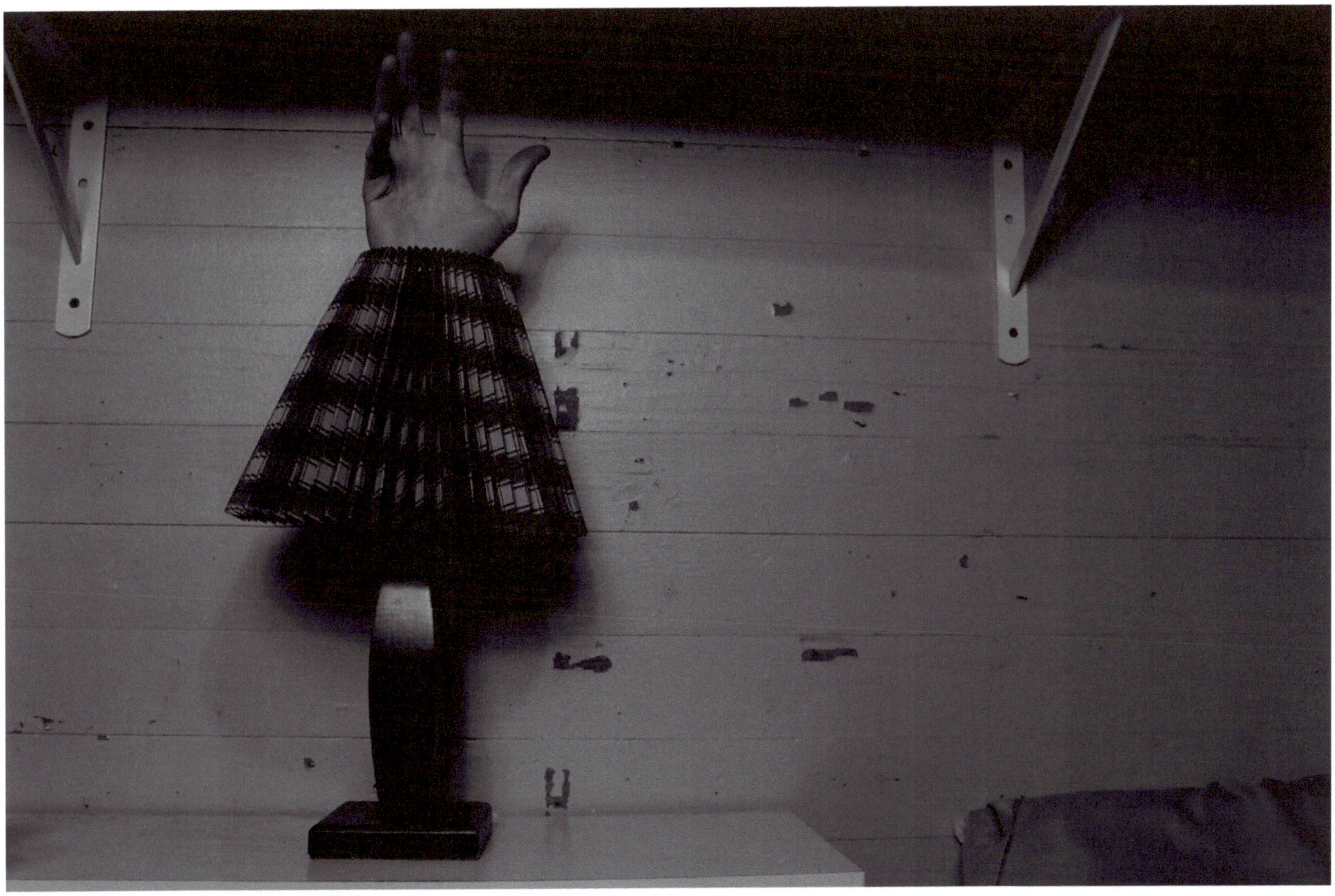

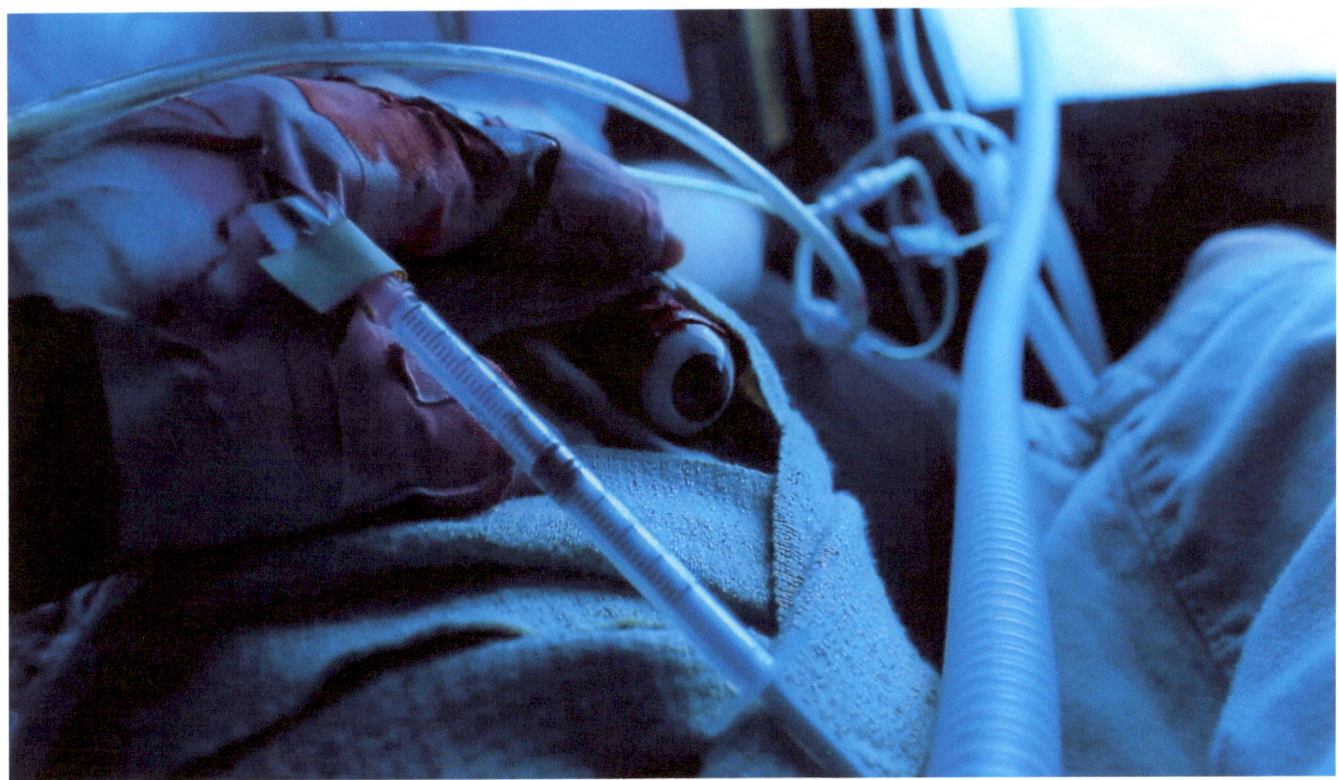

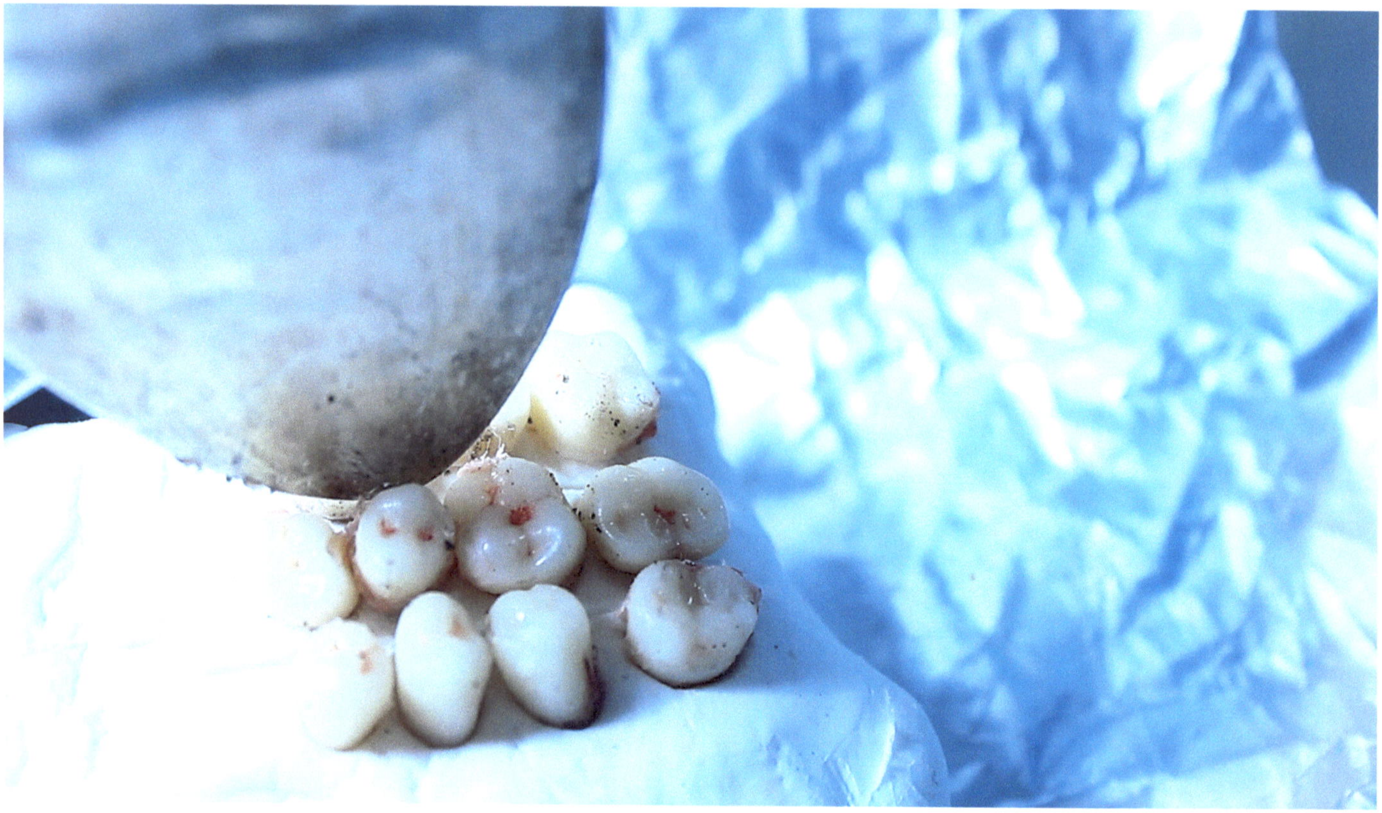

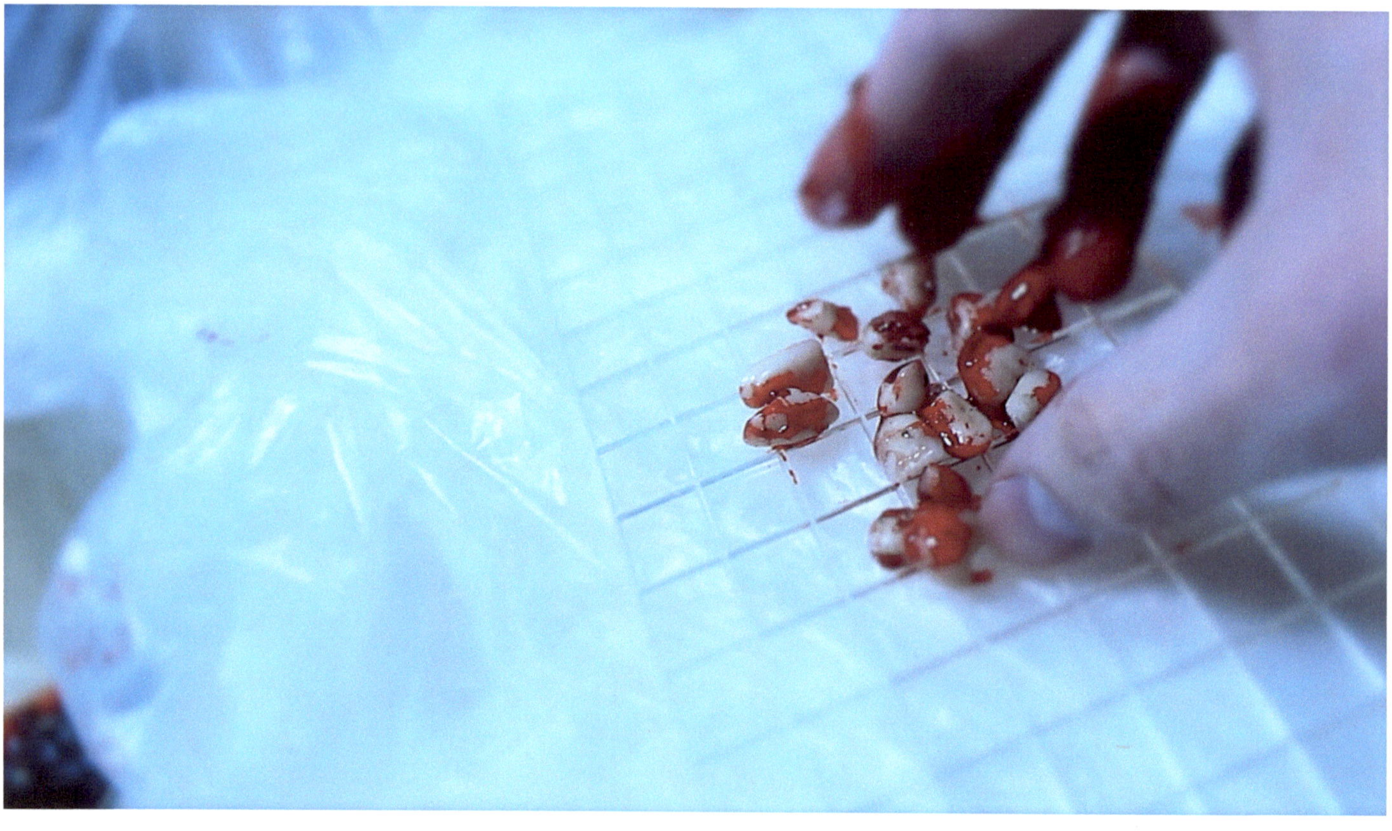

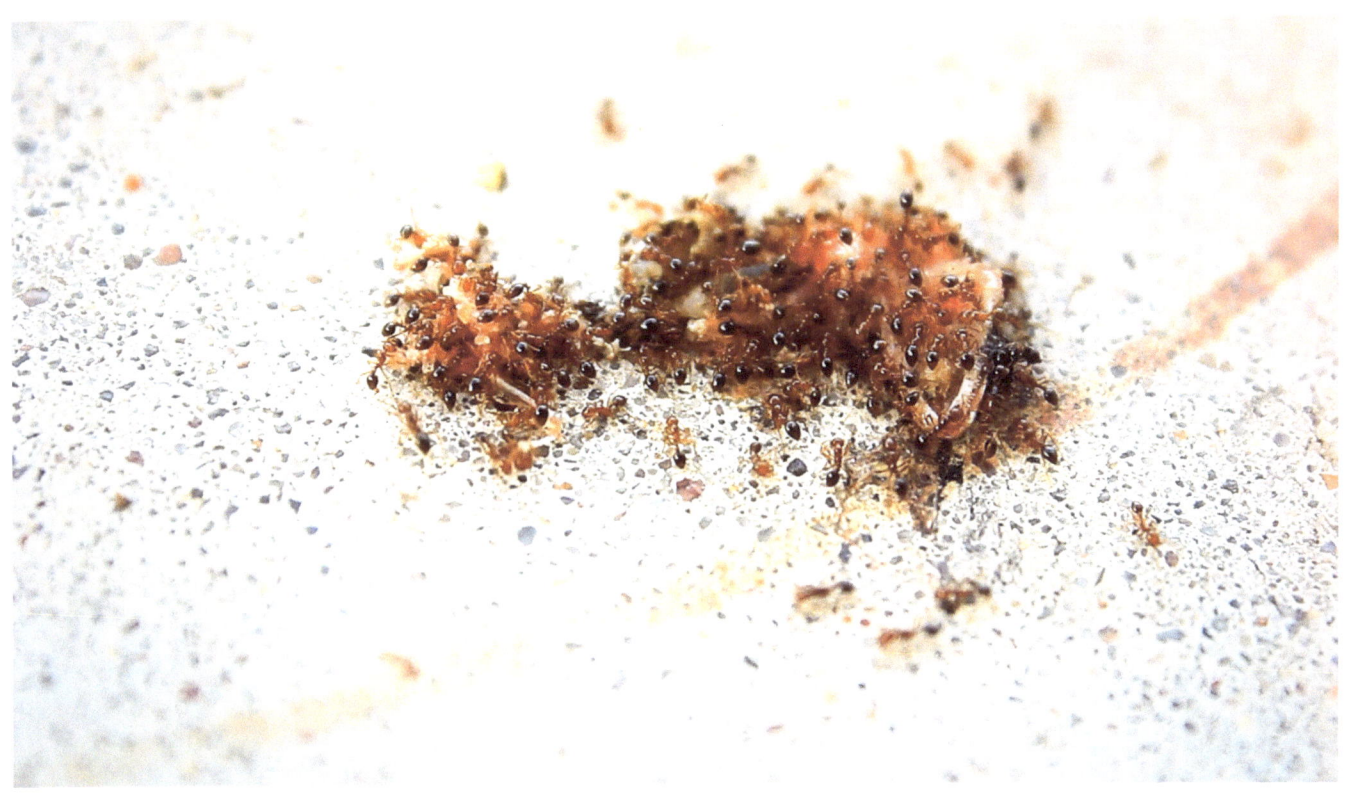

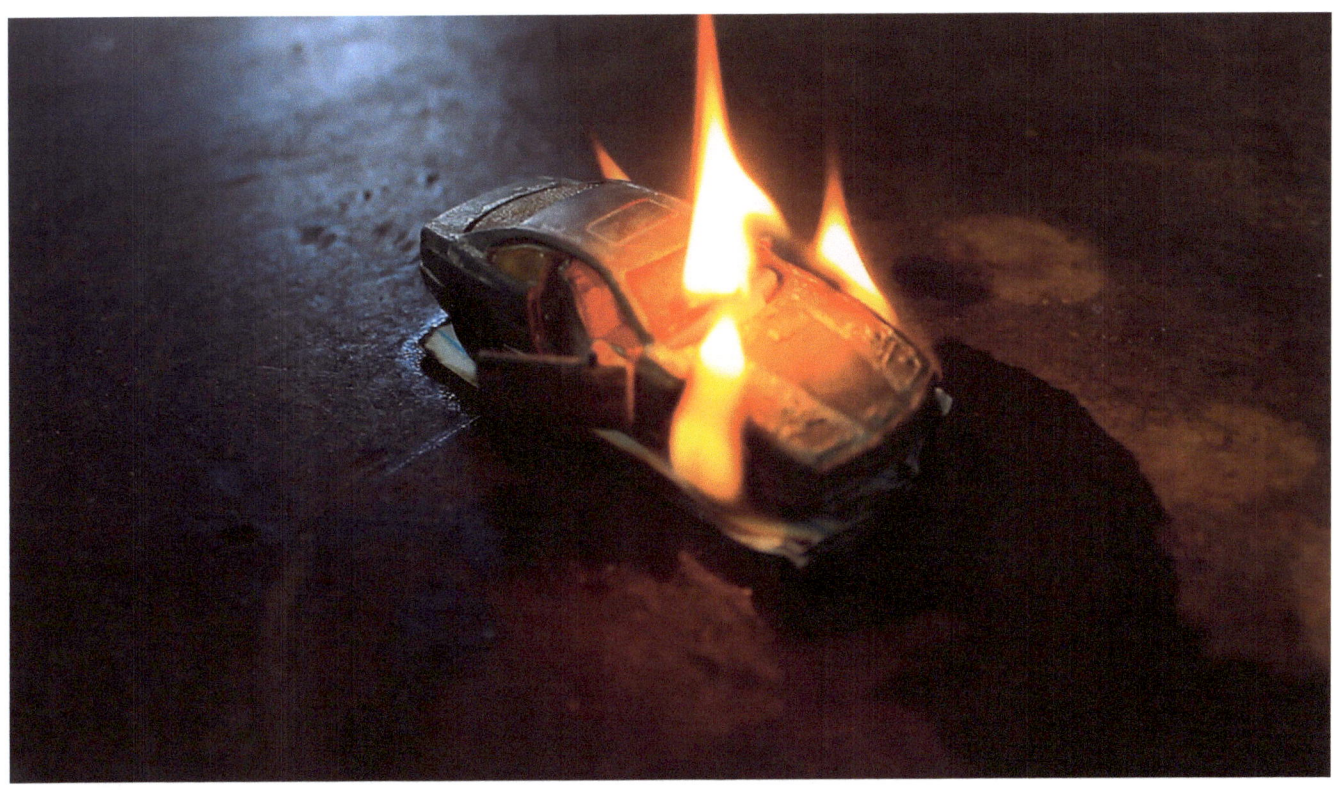

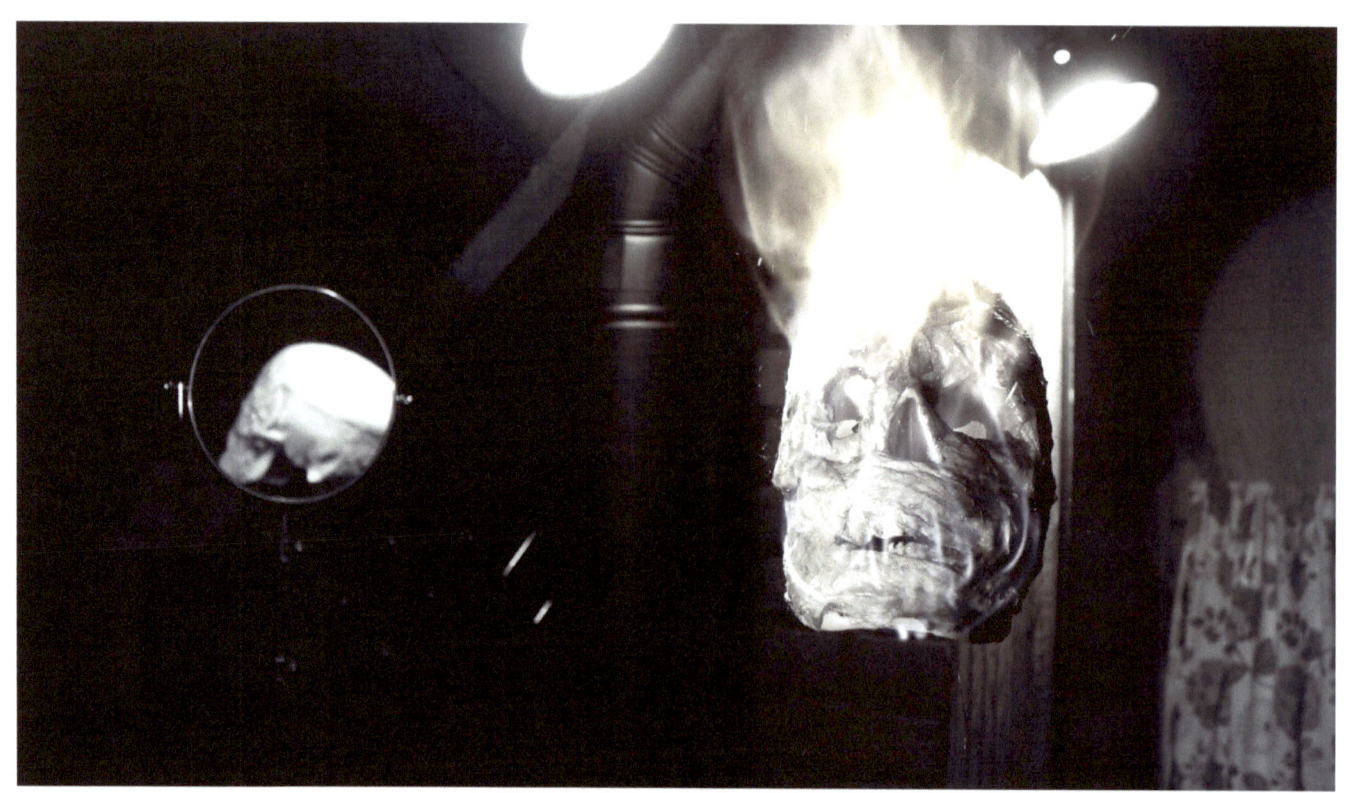
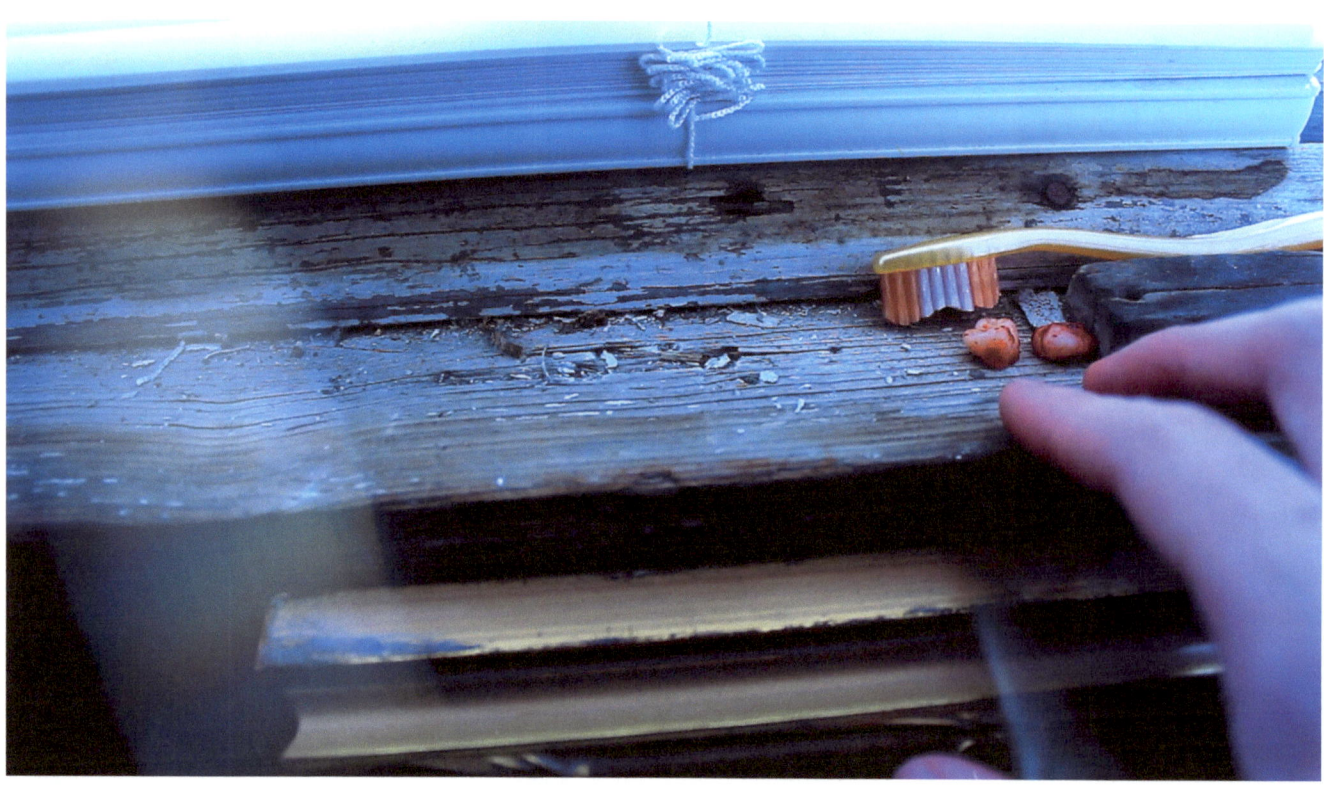

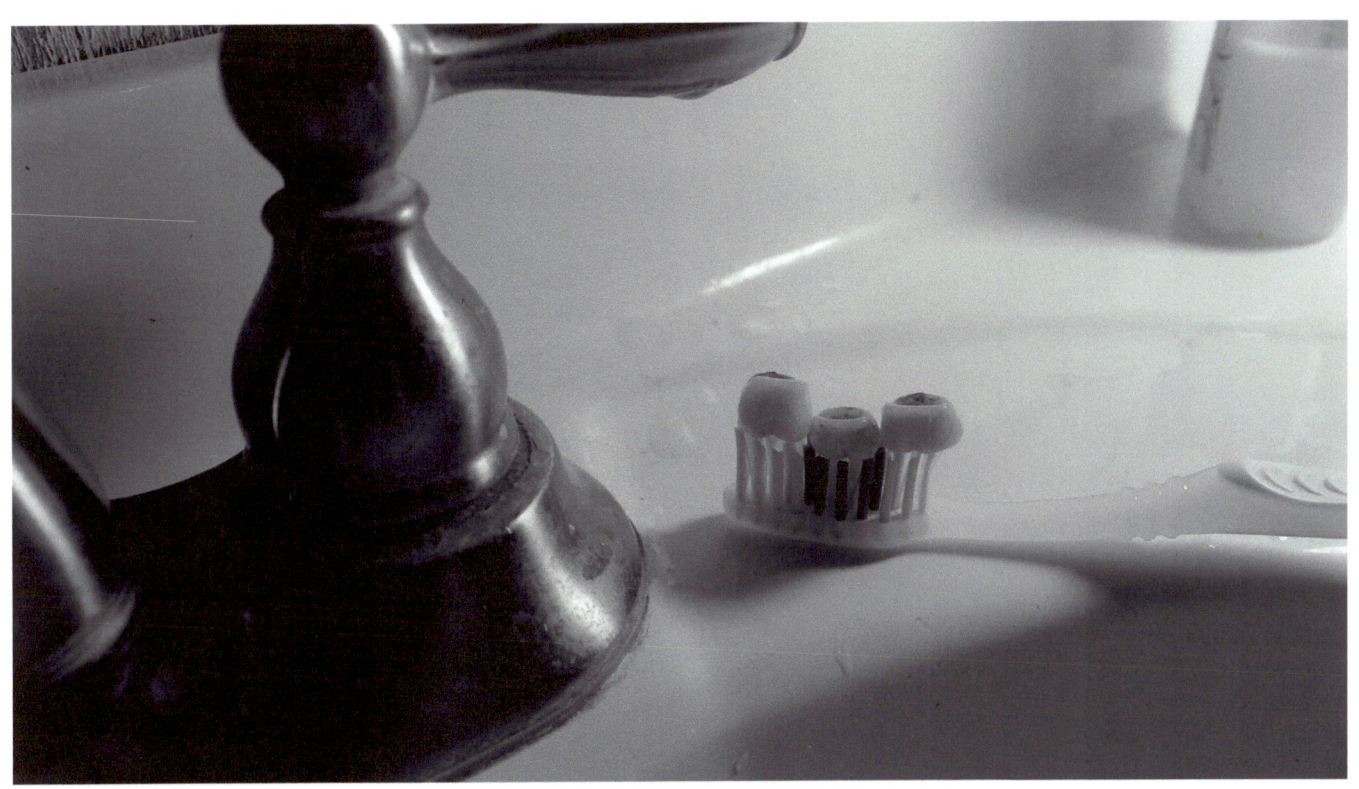
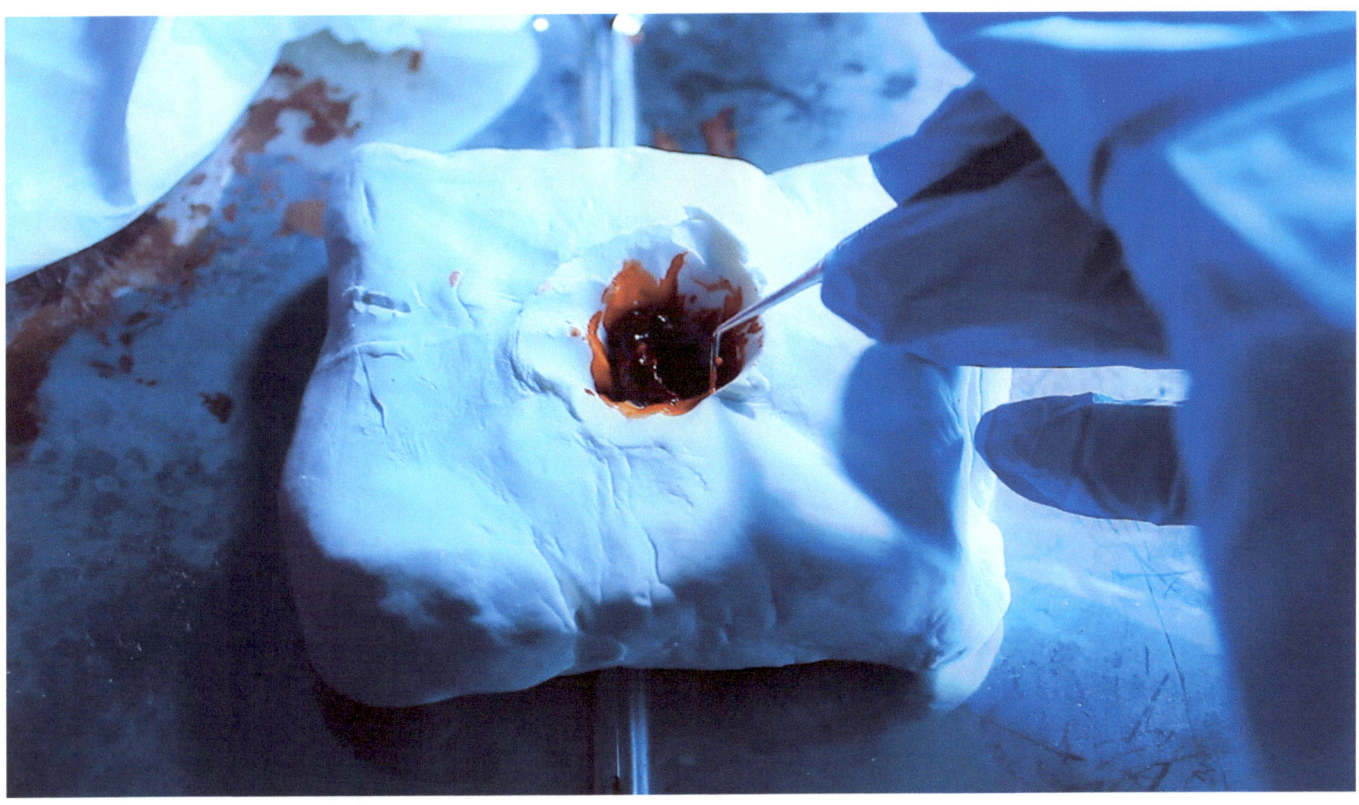

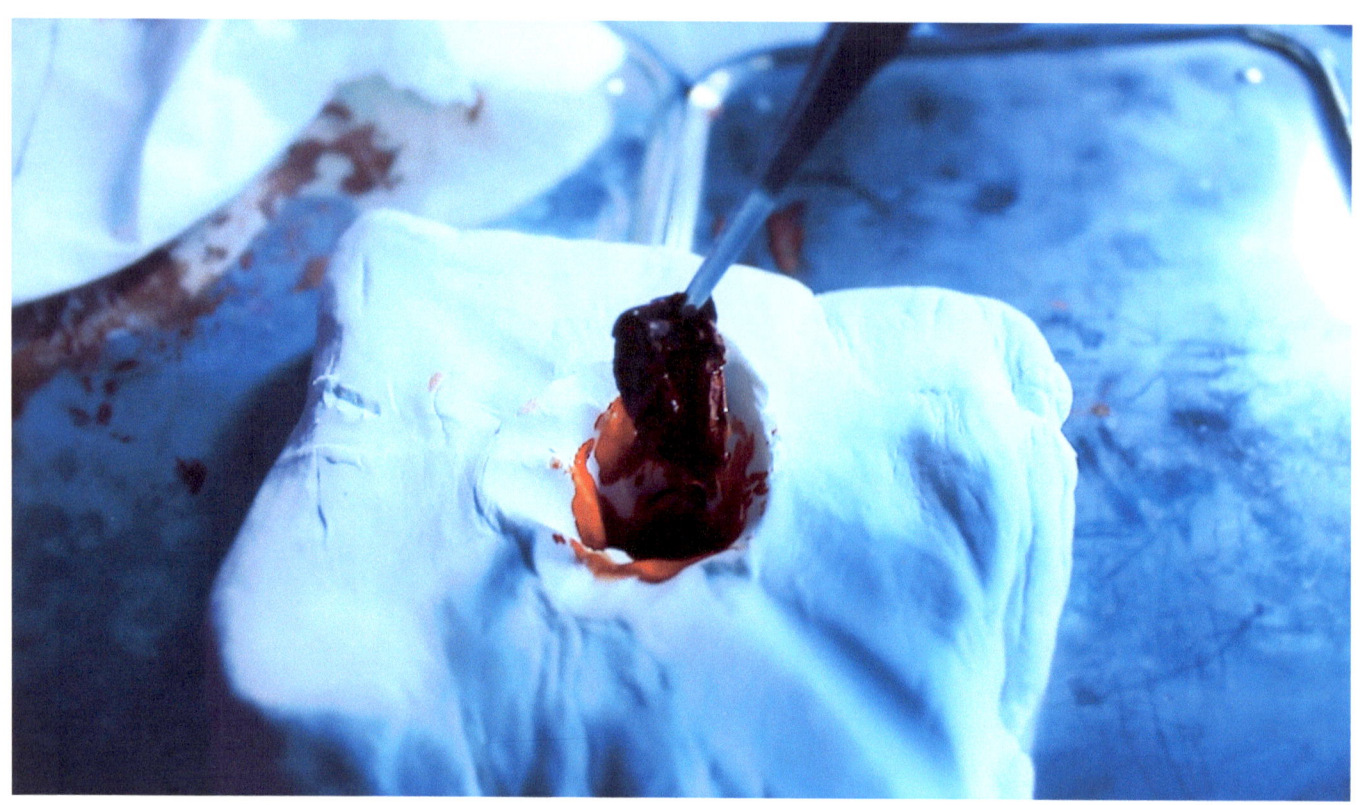

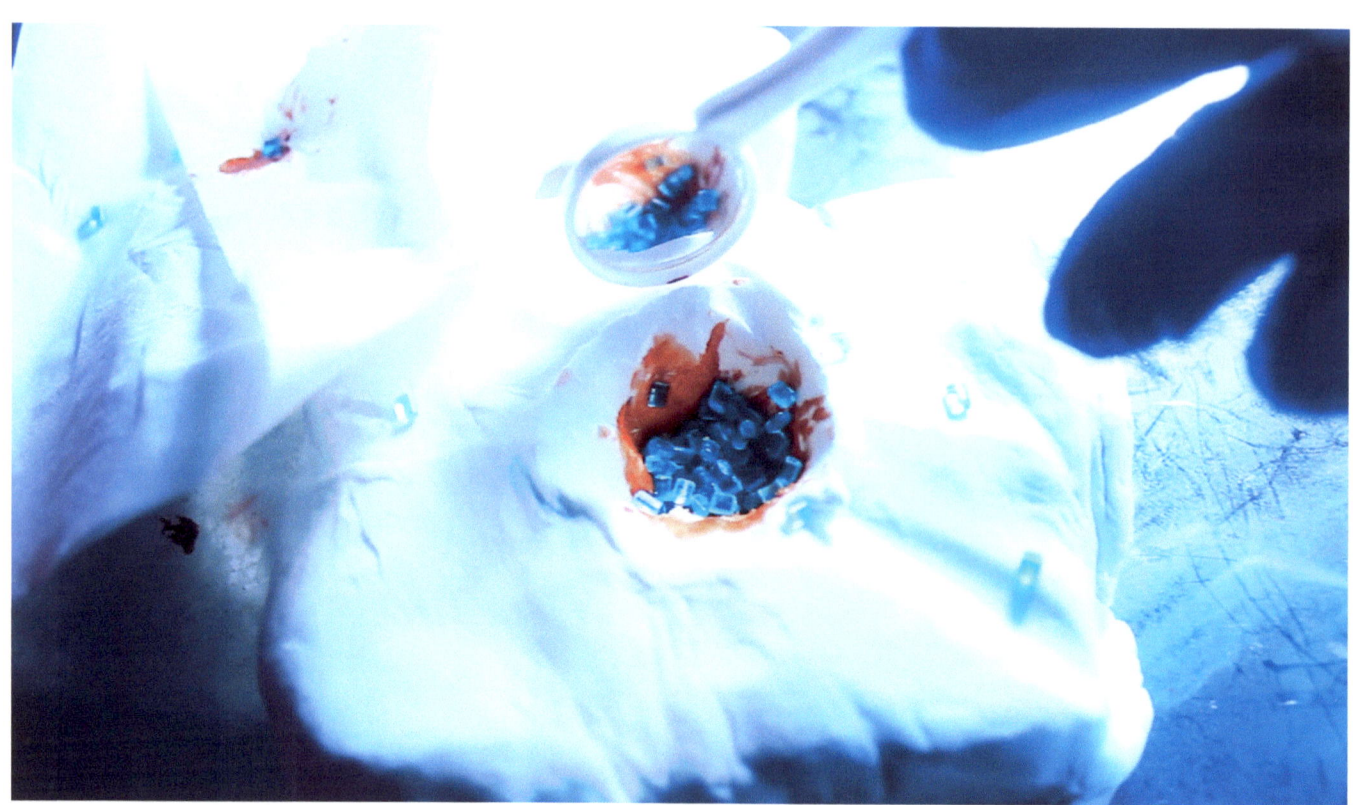

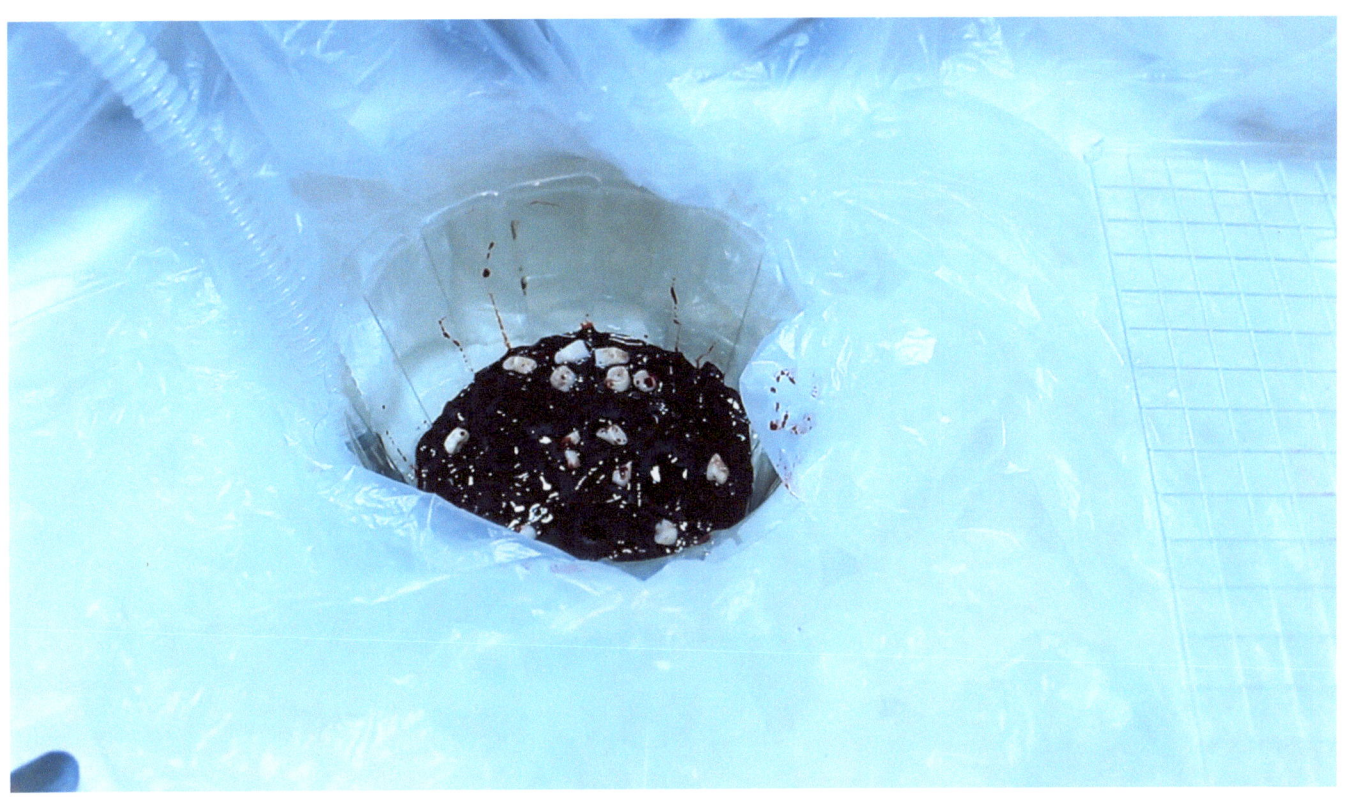
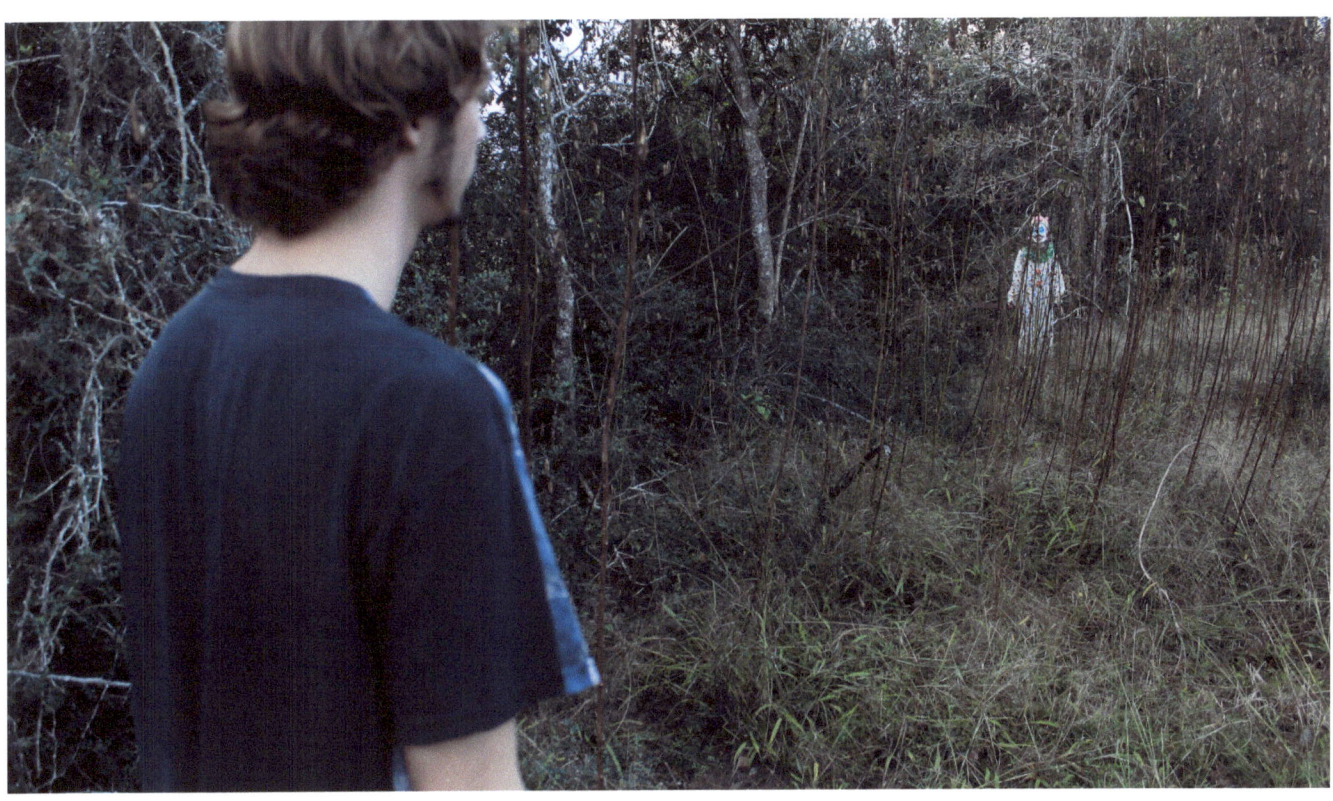

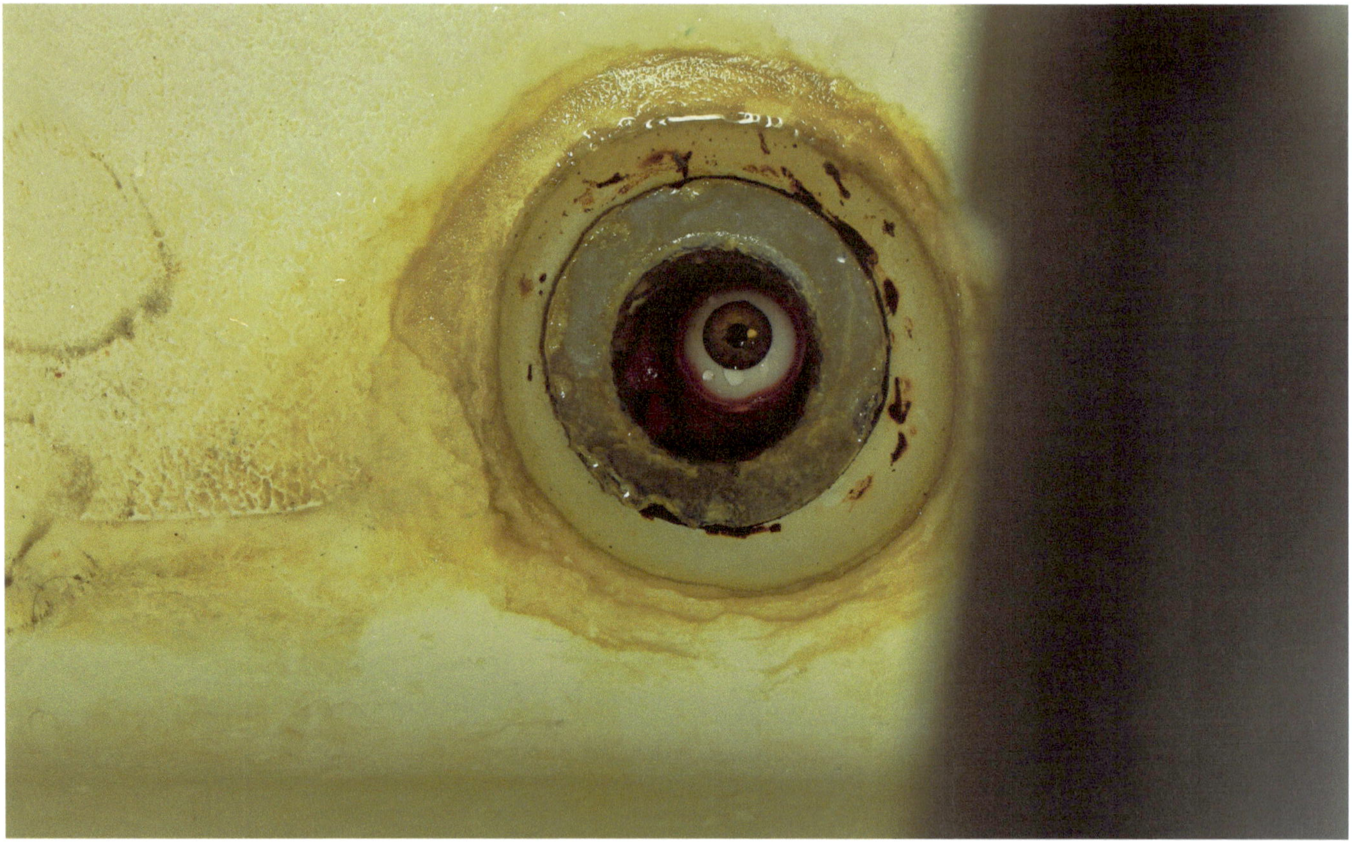

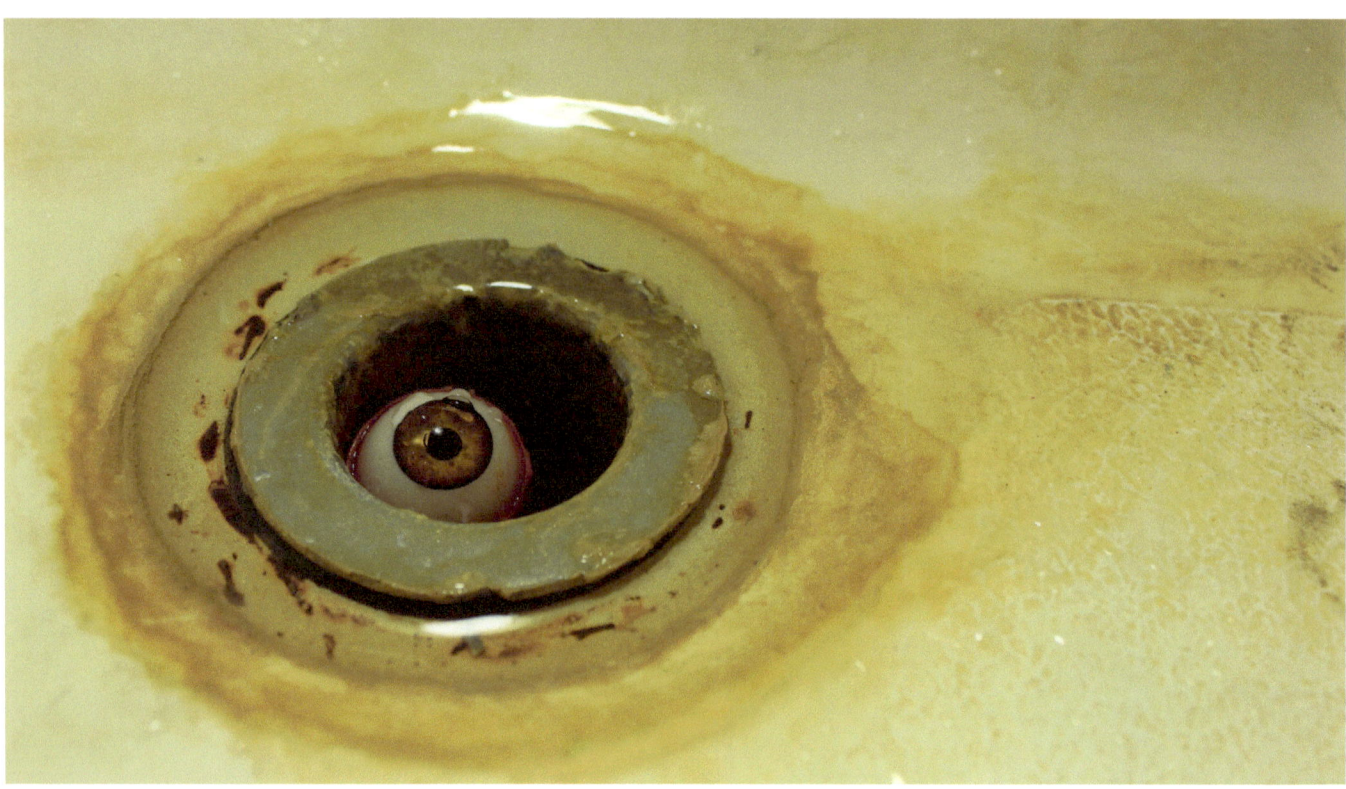

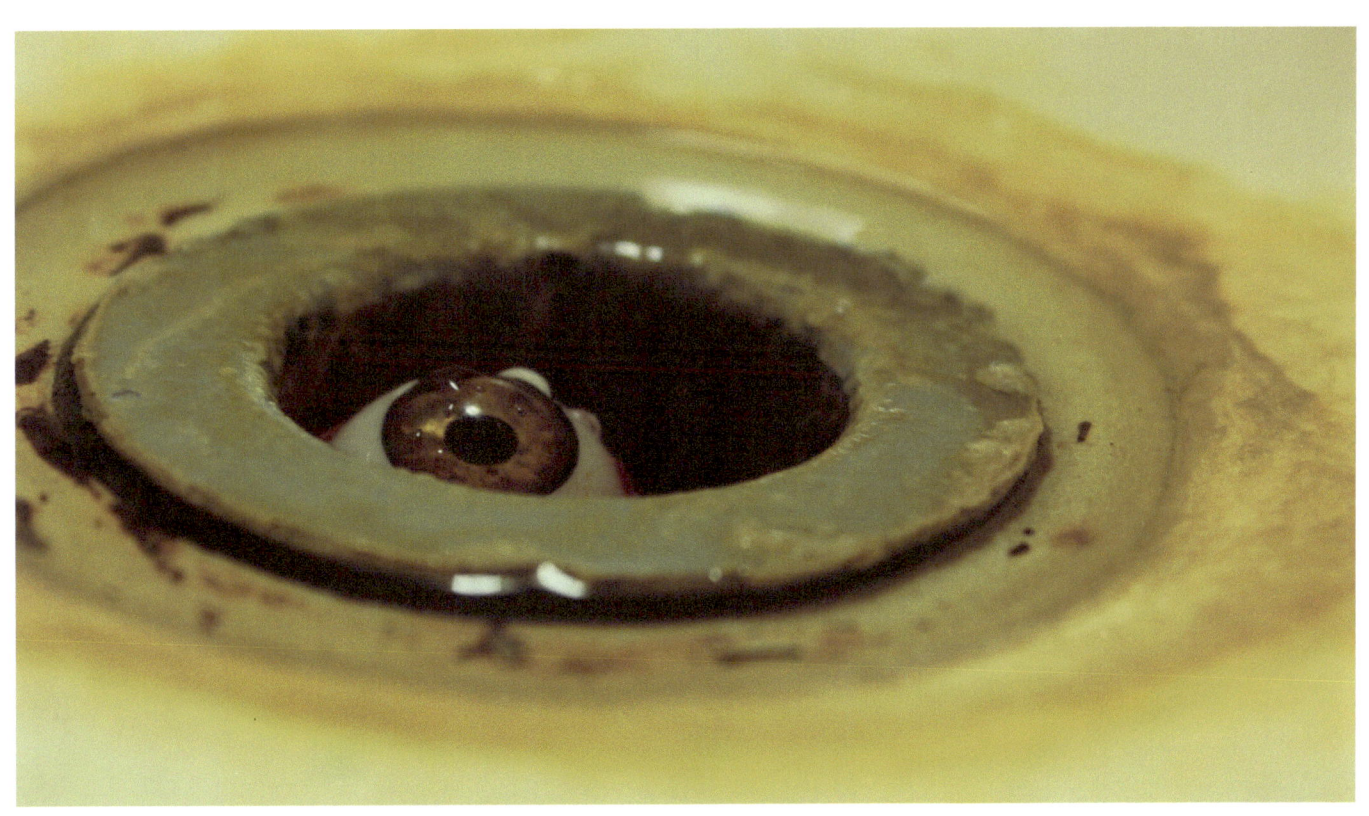

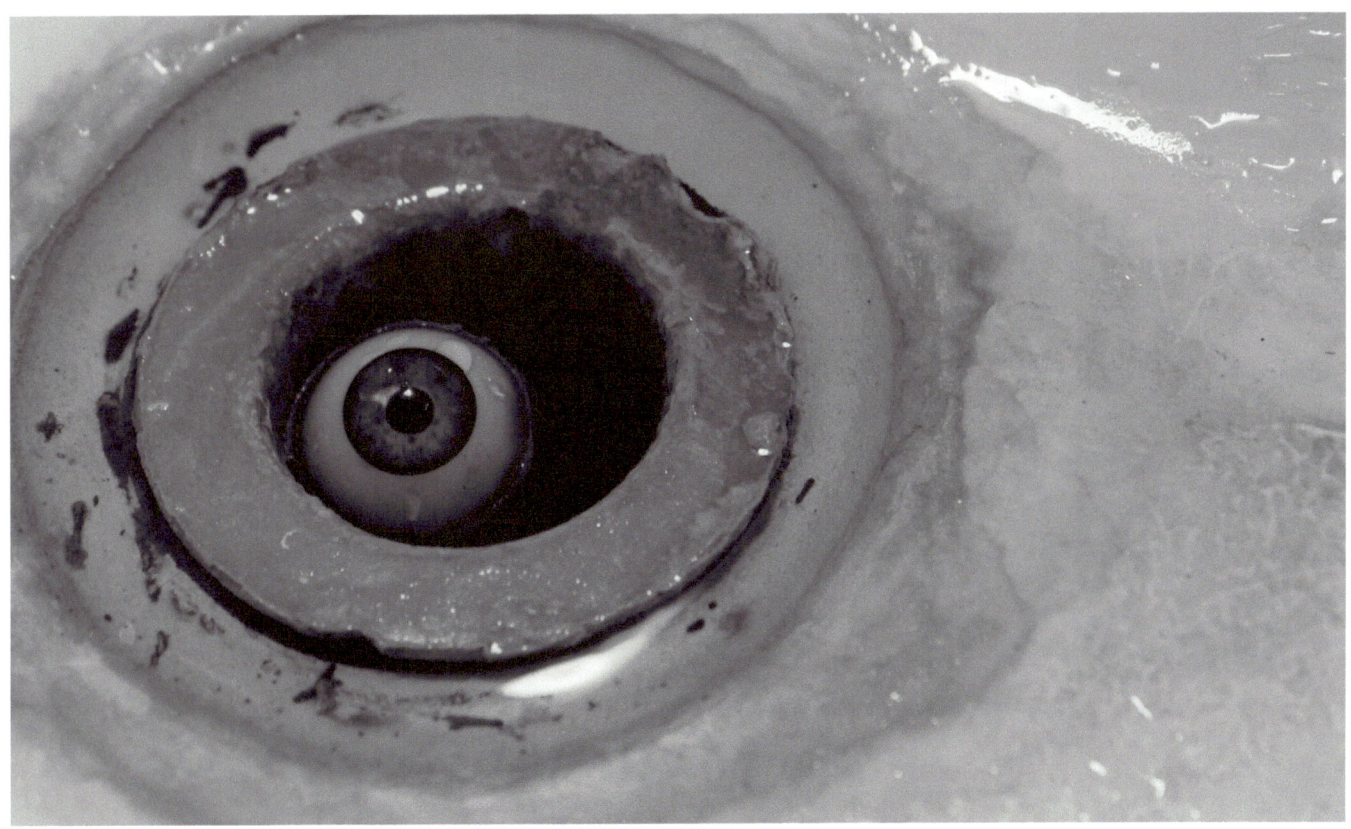

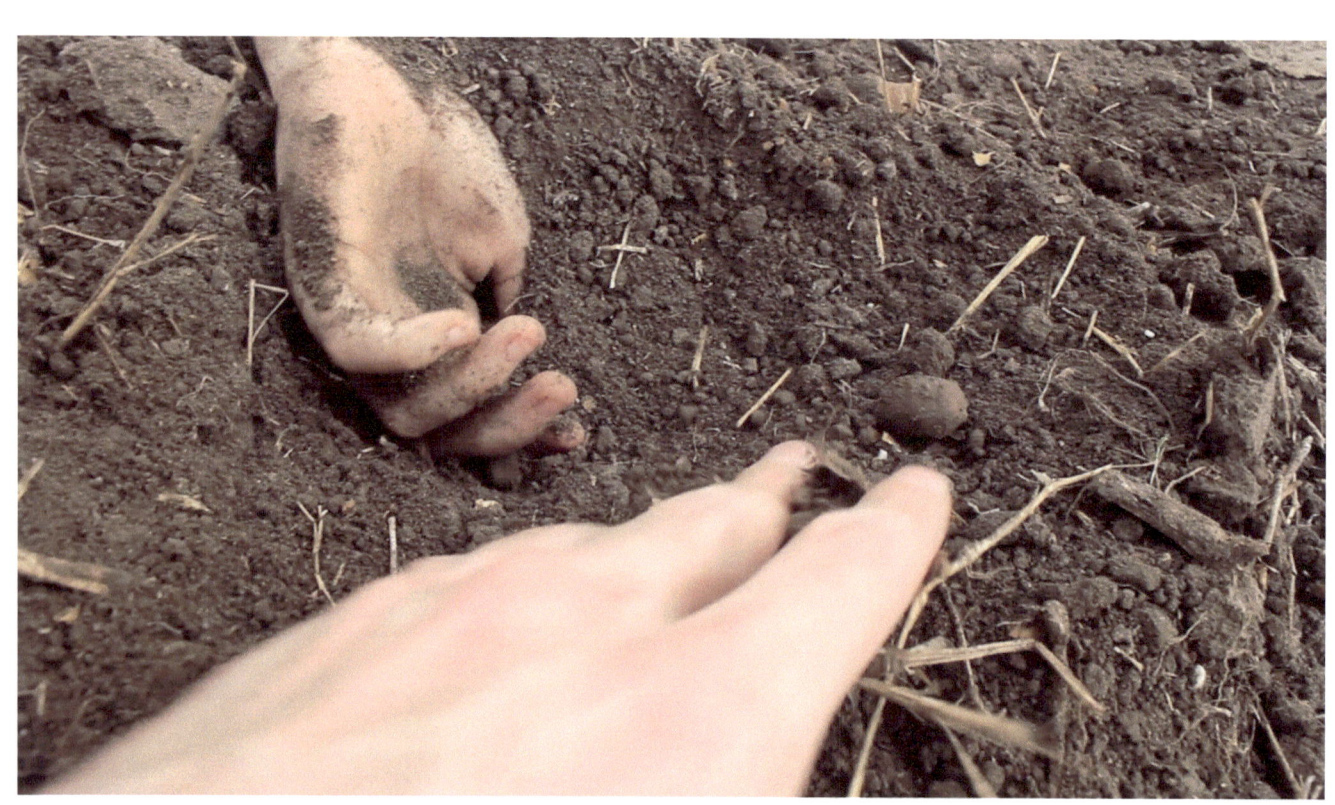

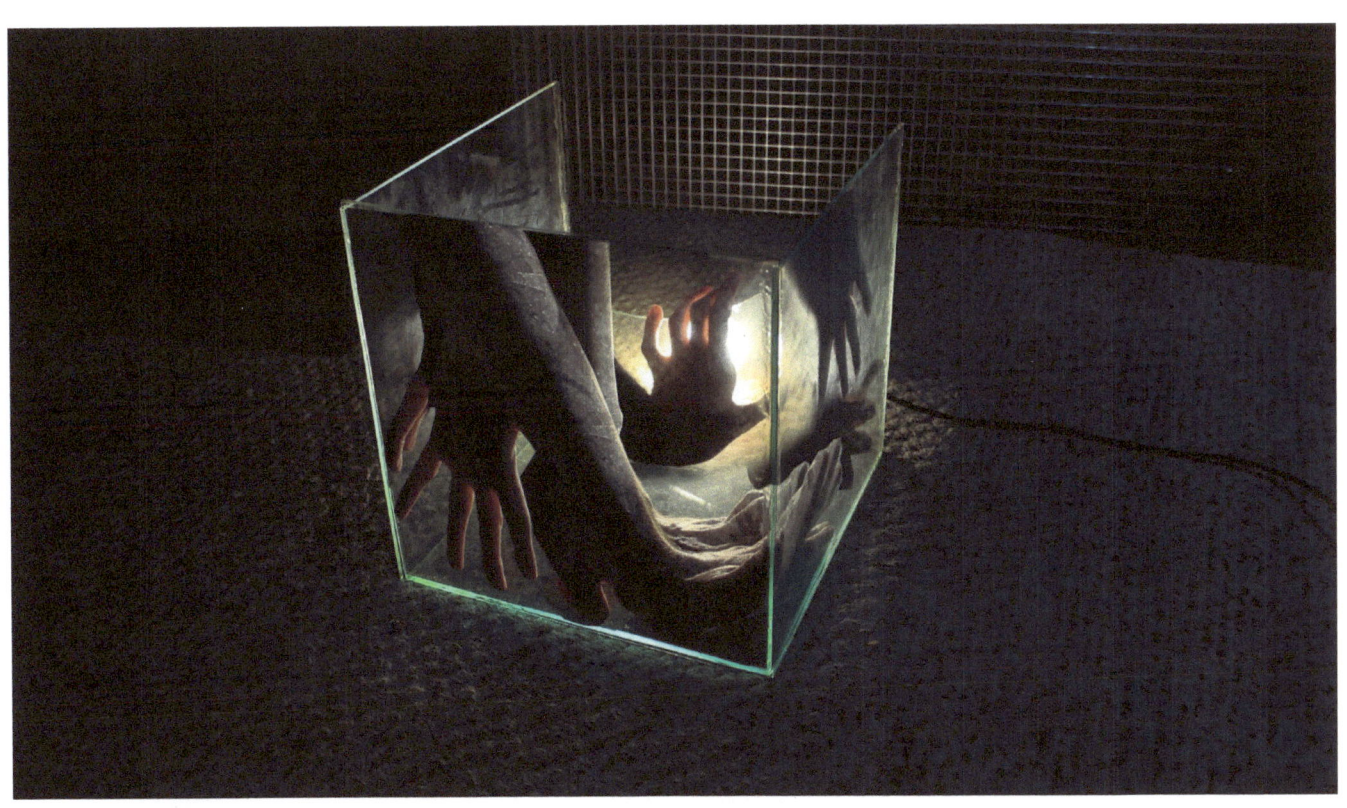

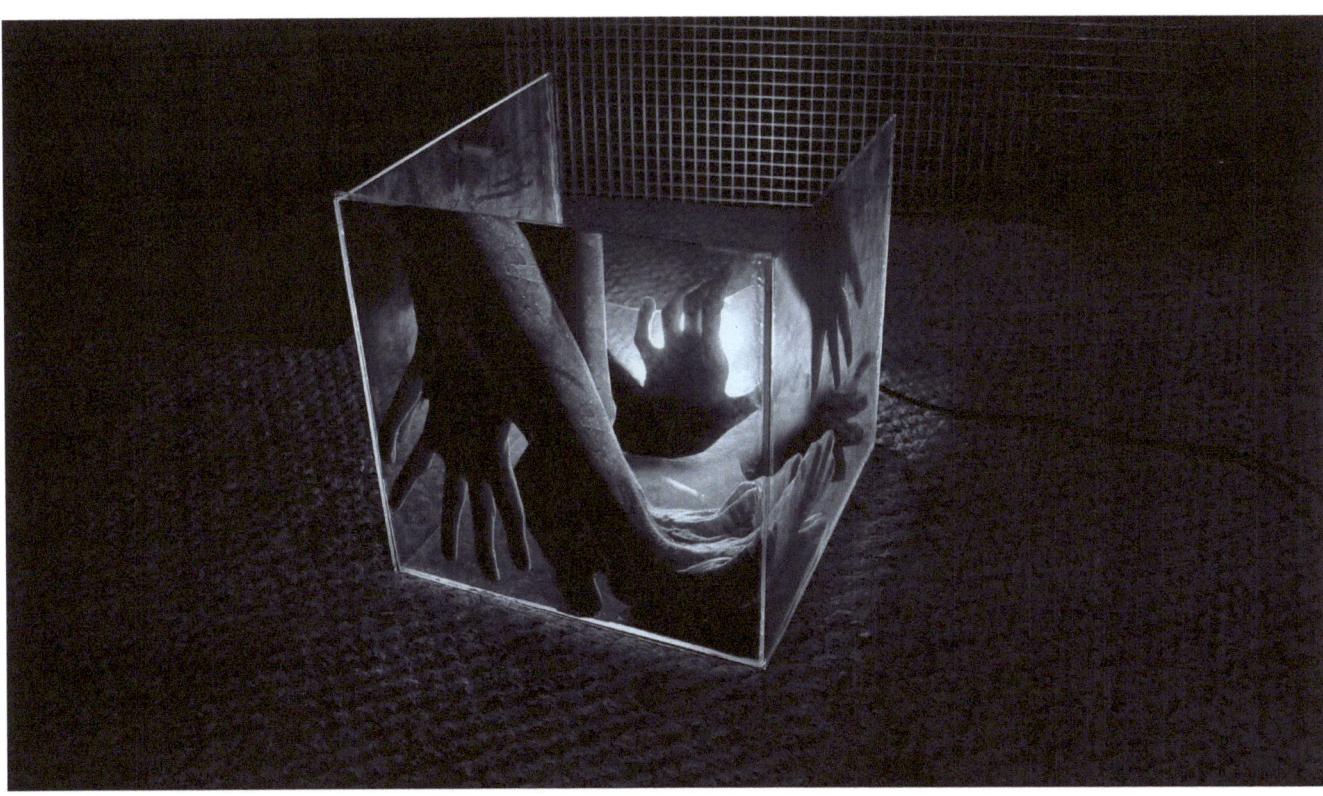

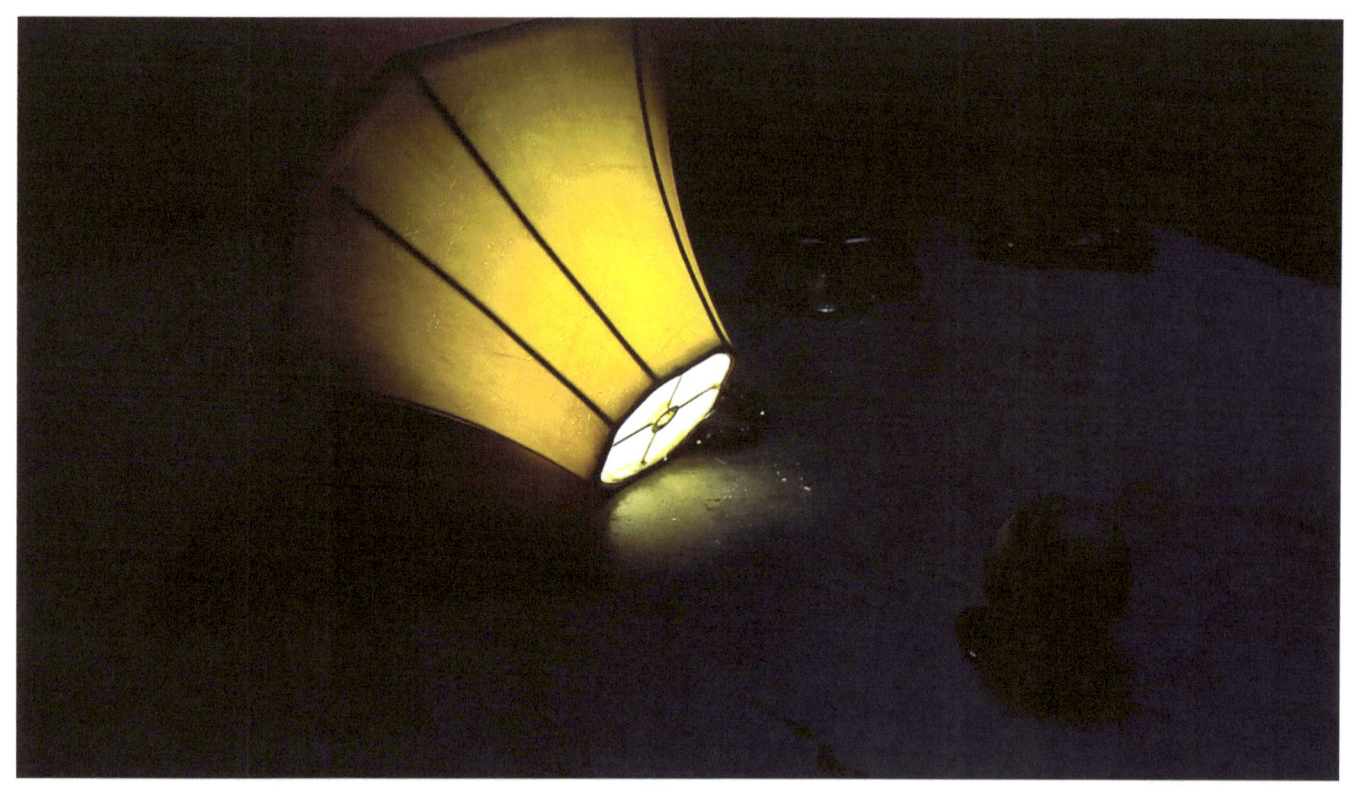

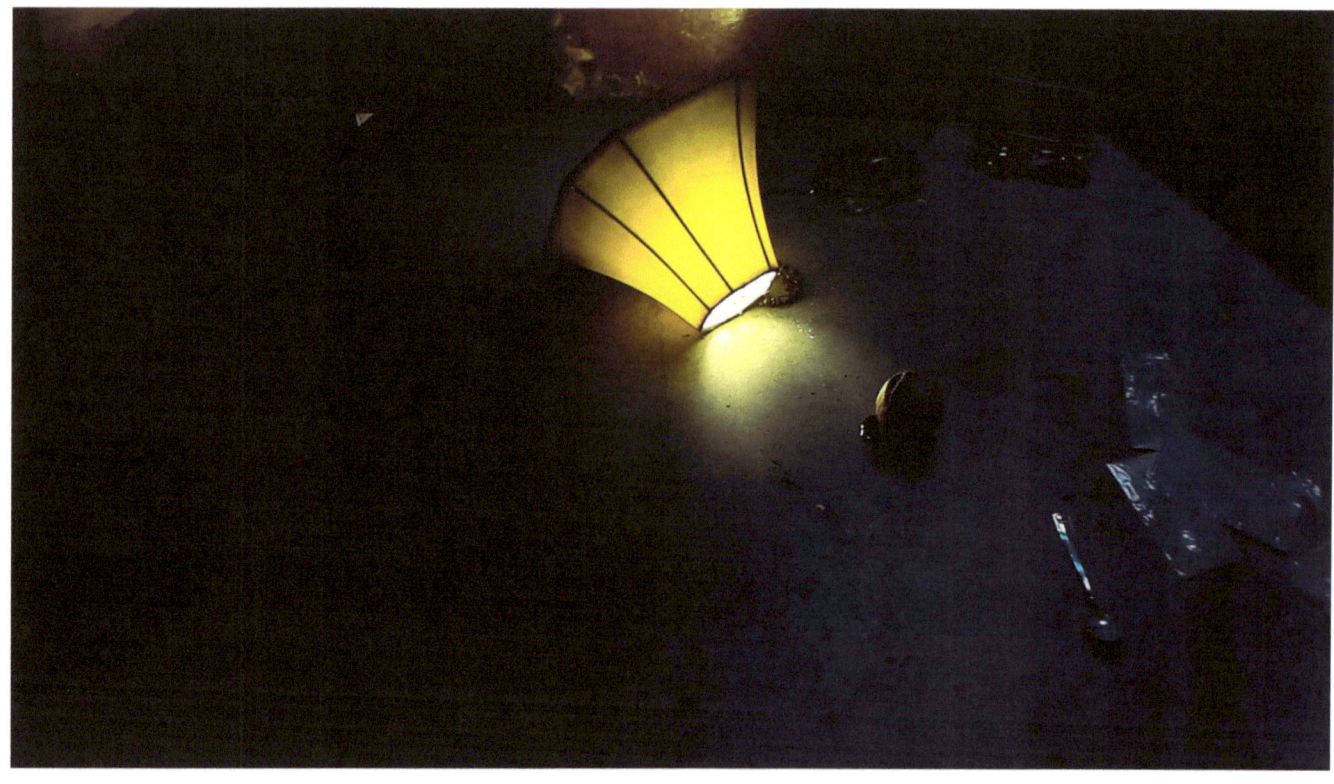

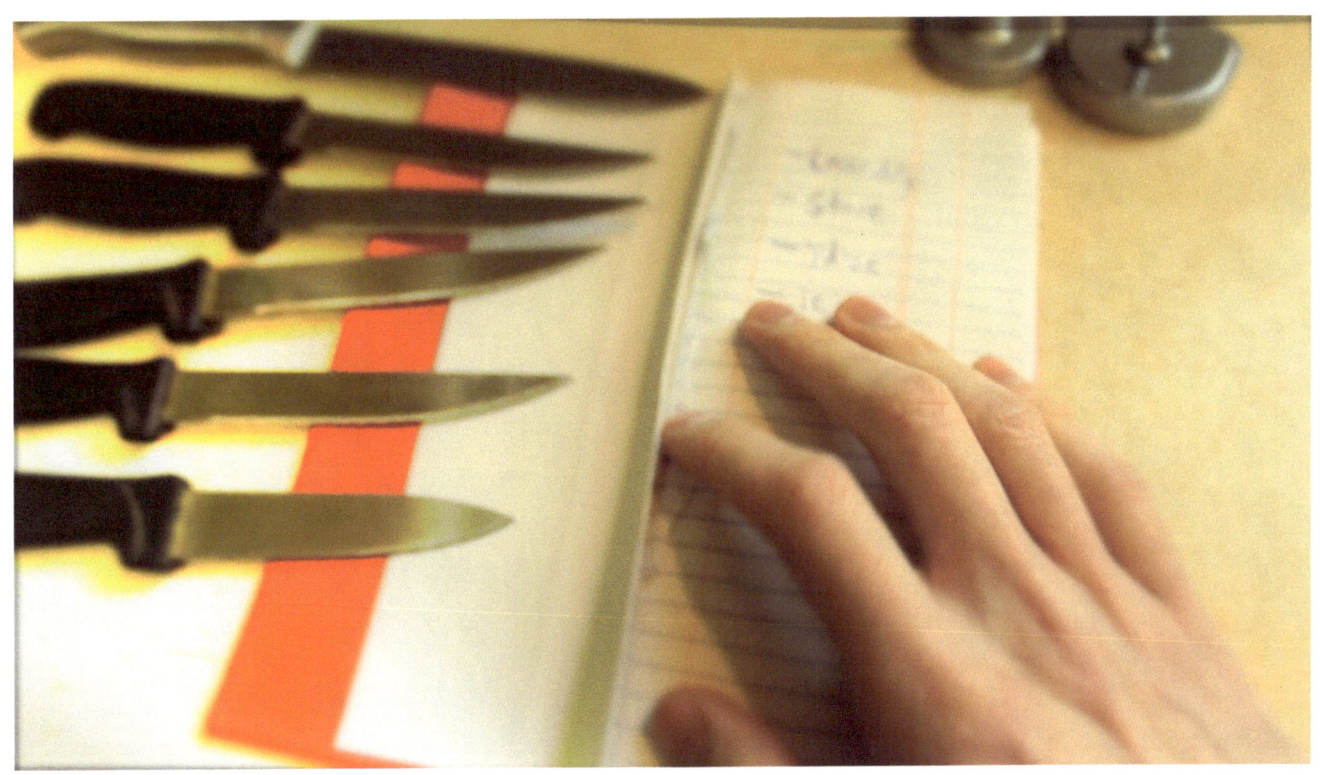

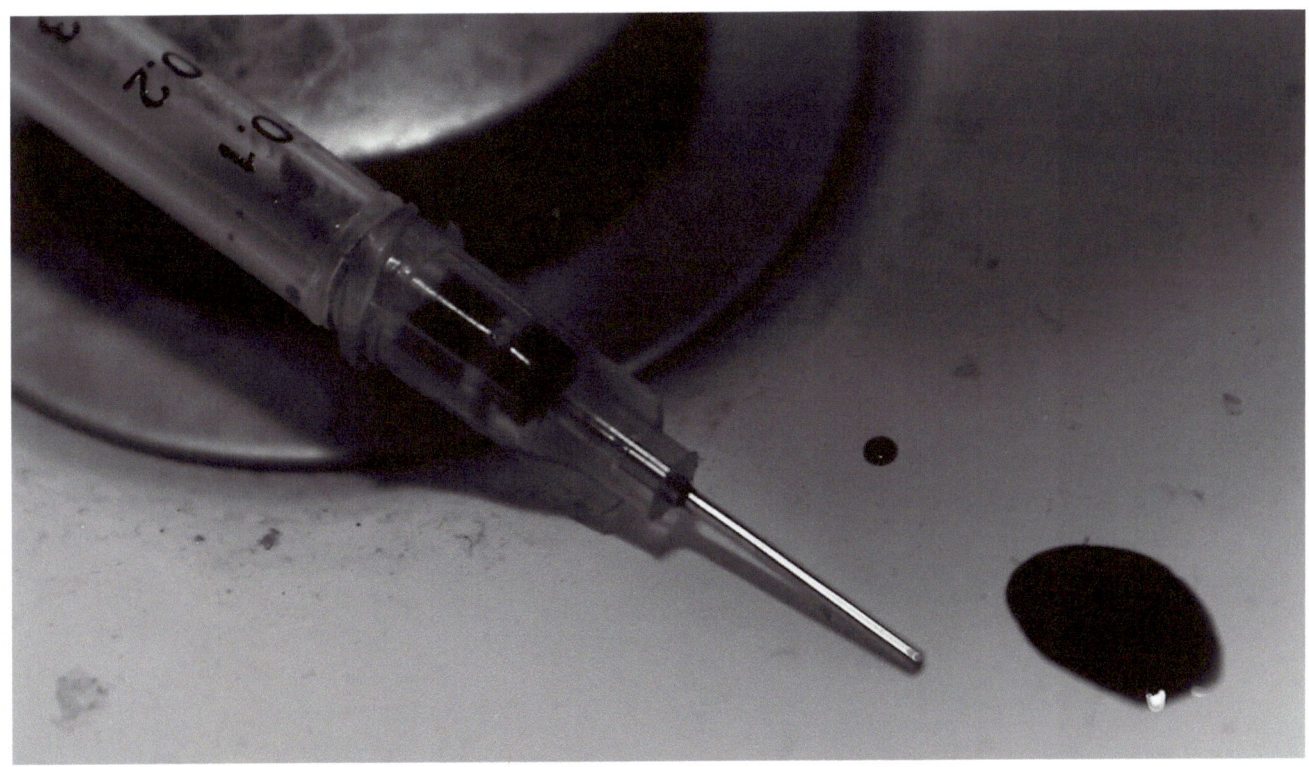

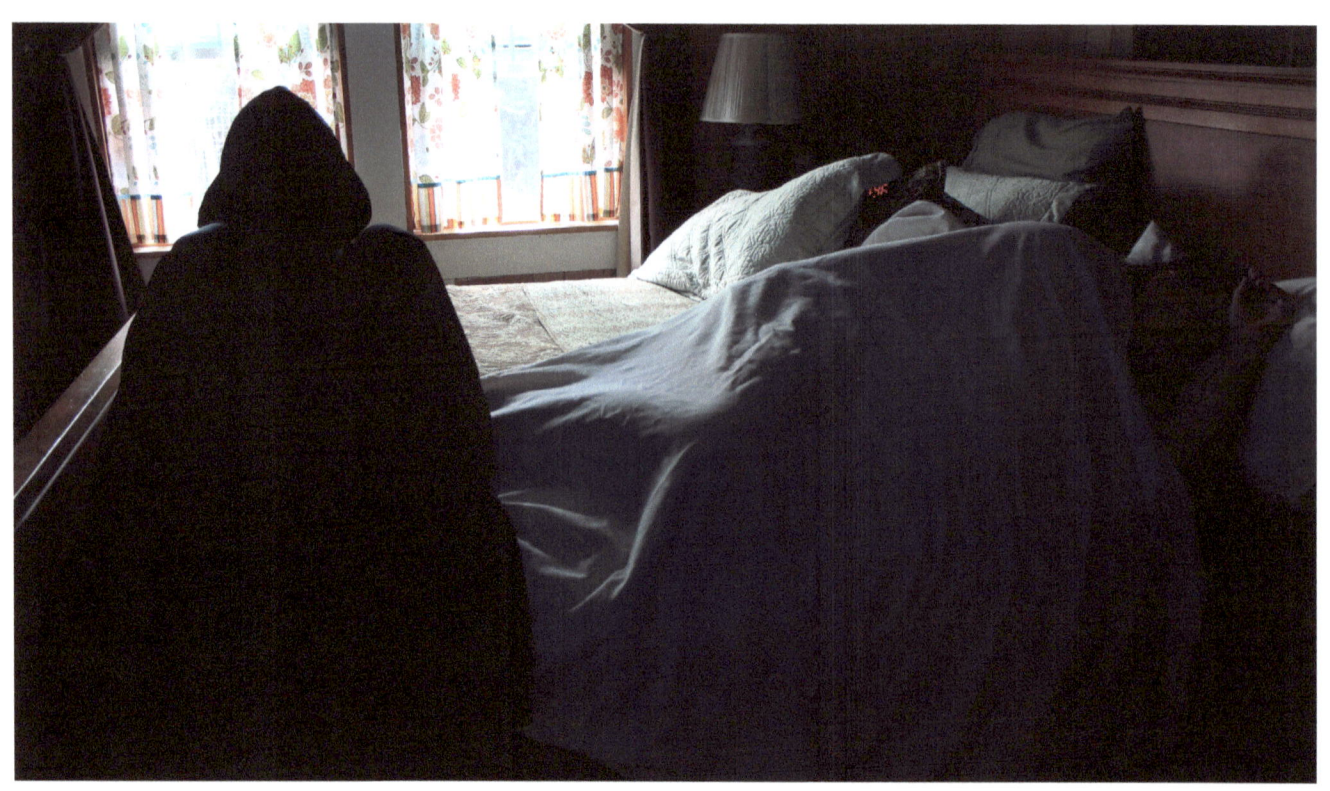

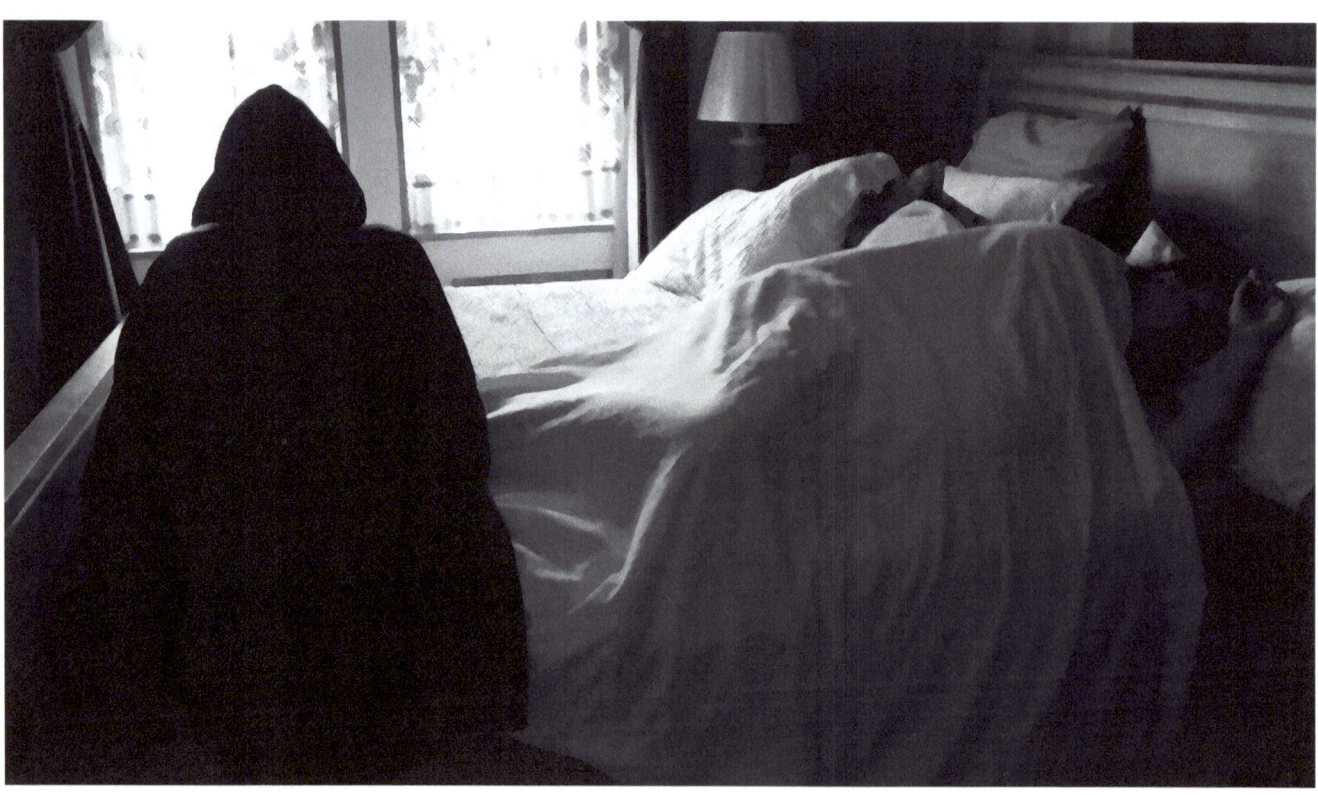

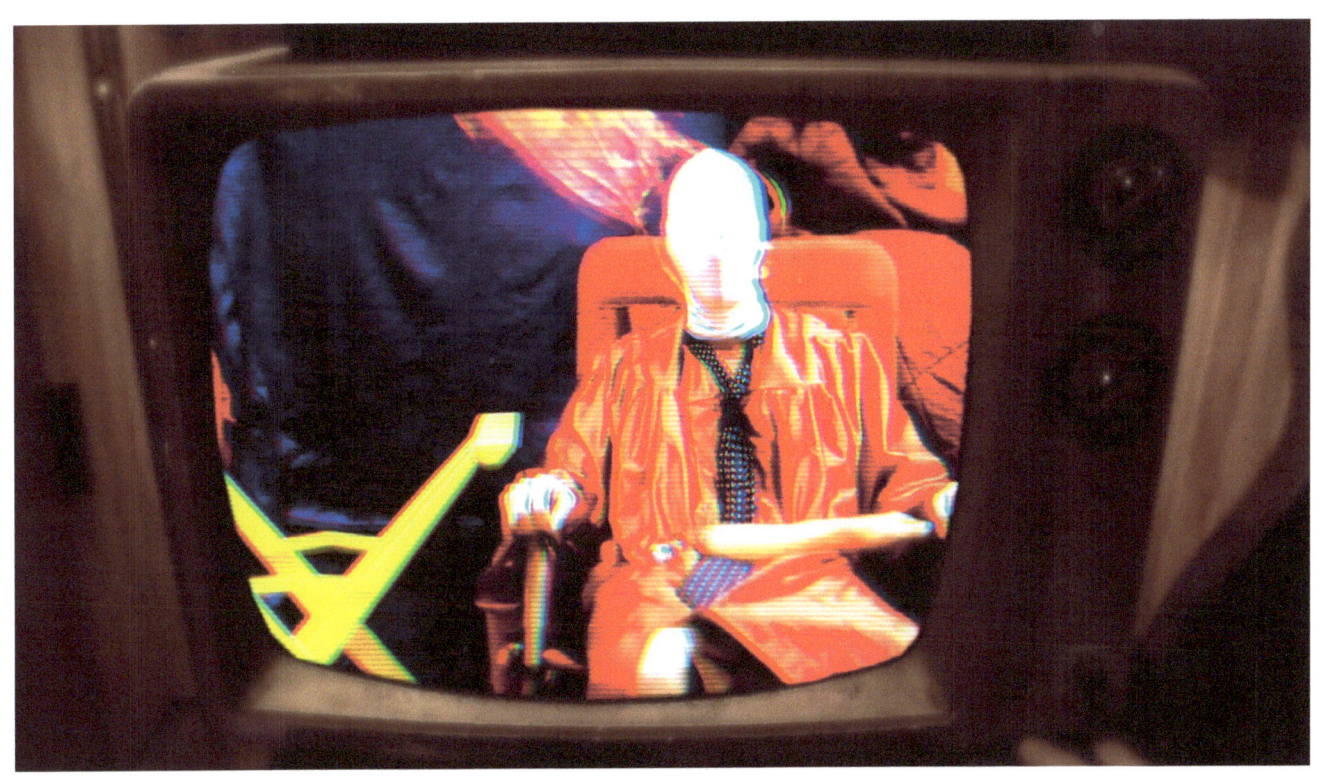
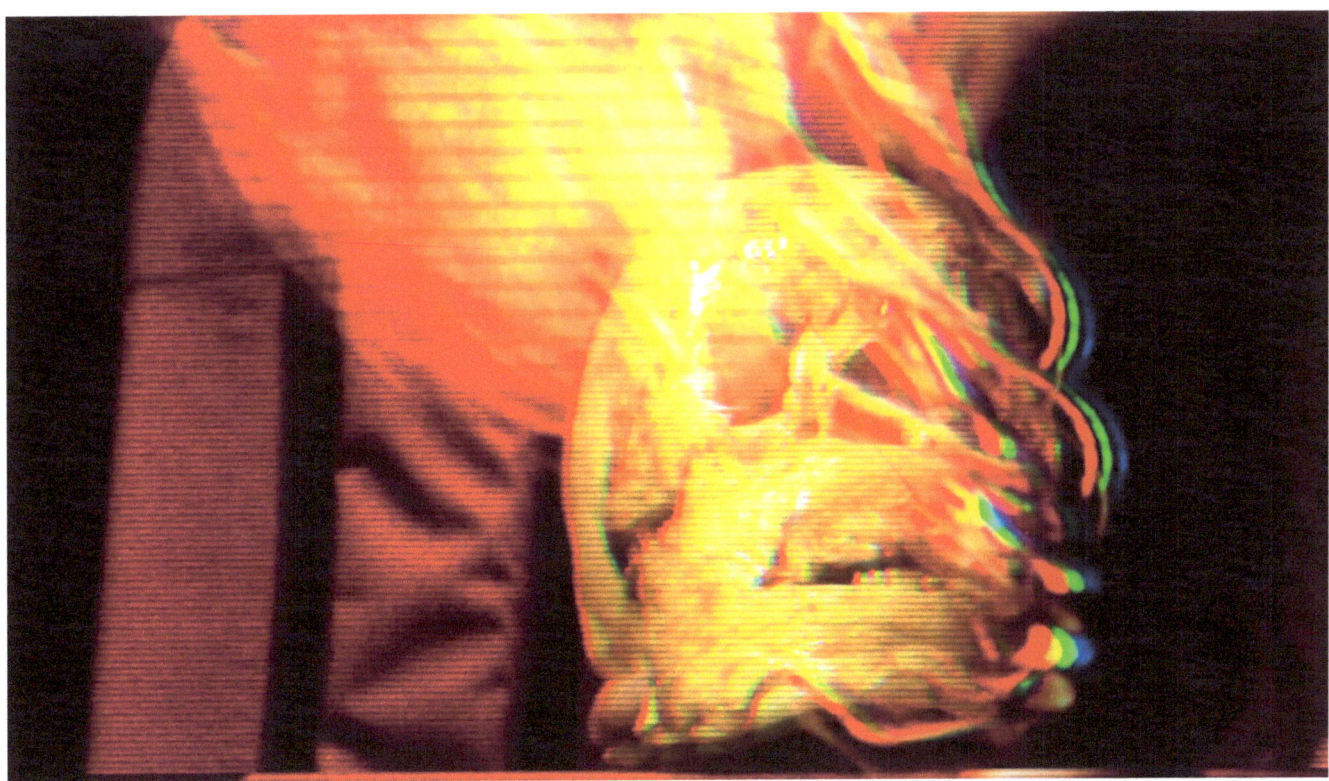

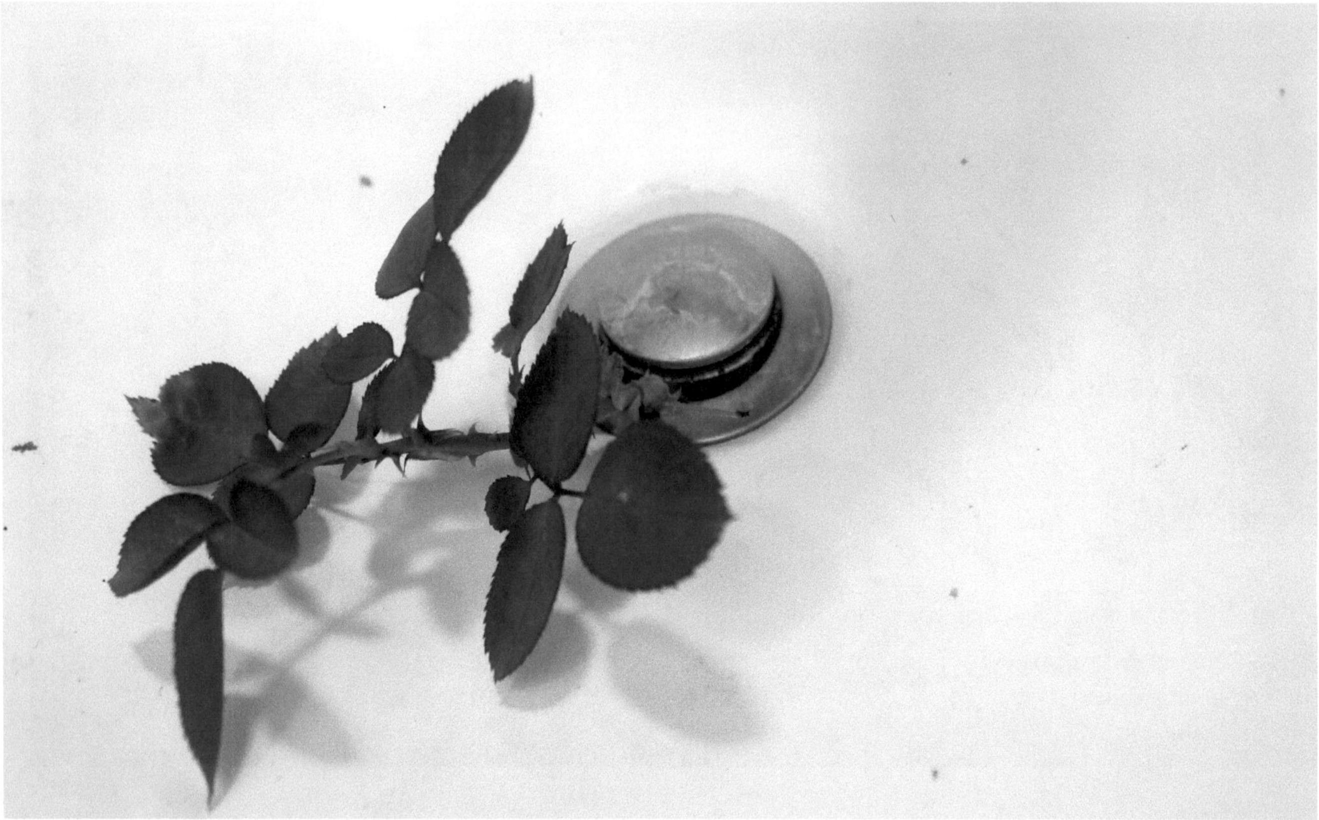

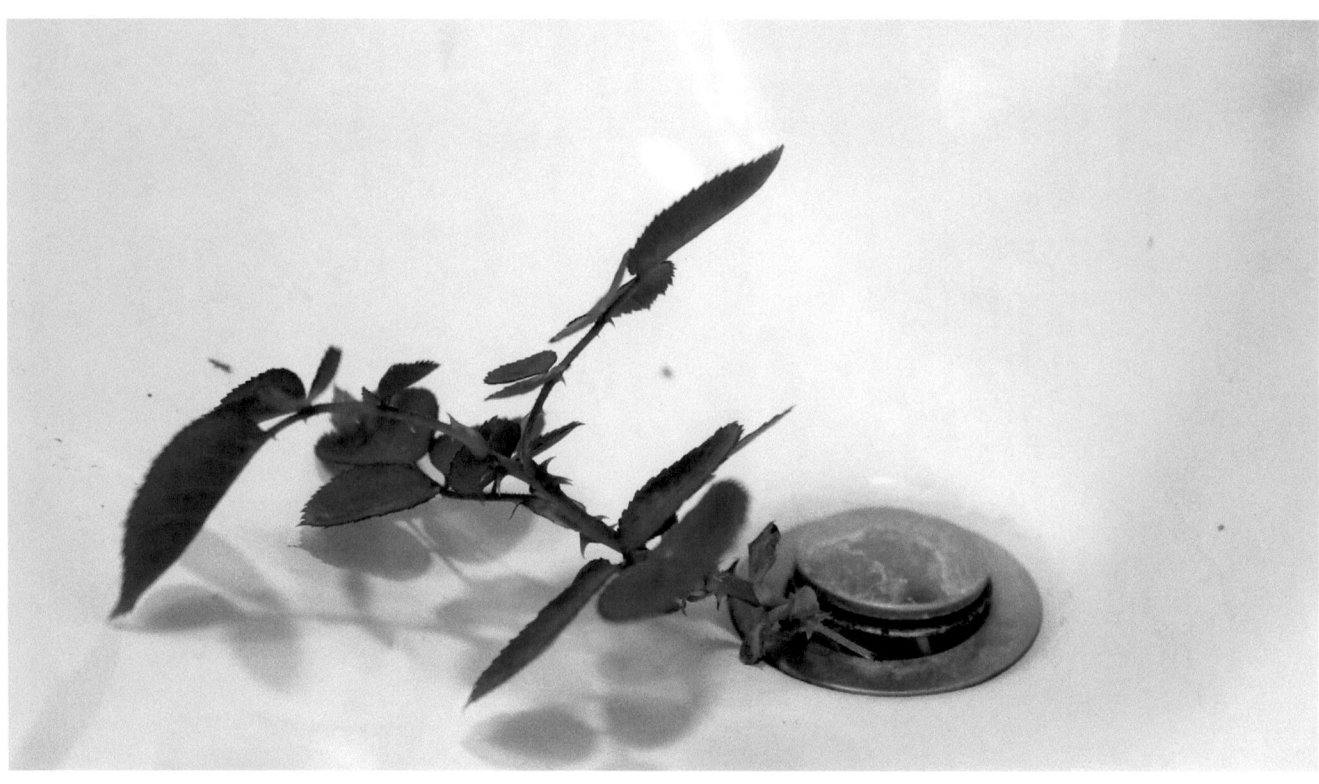

Visions.

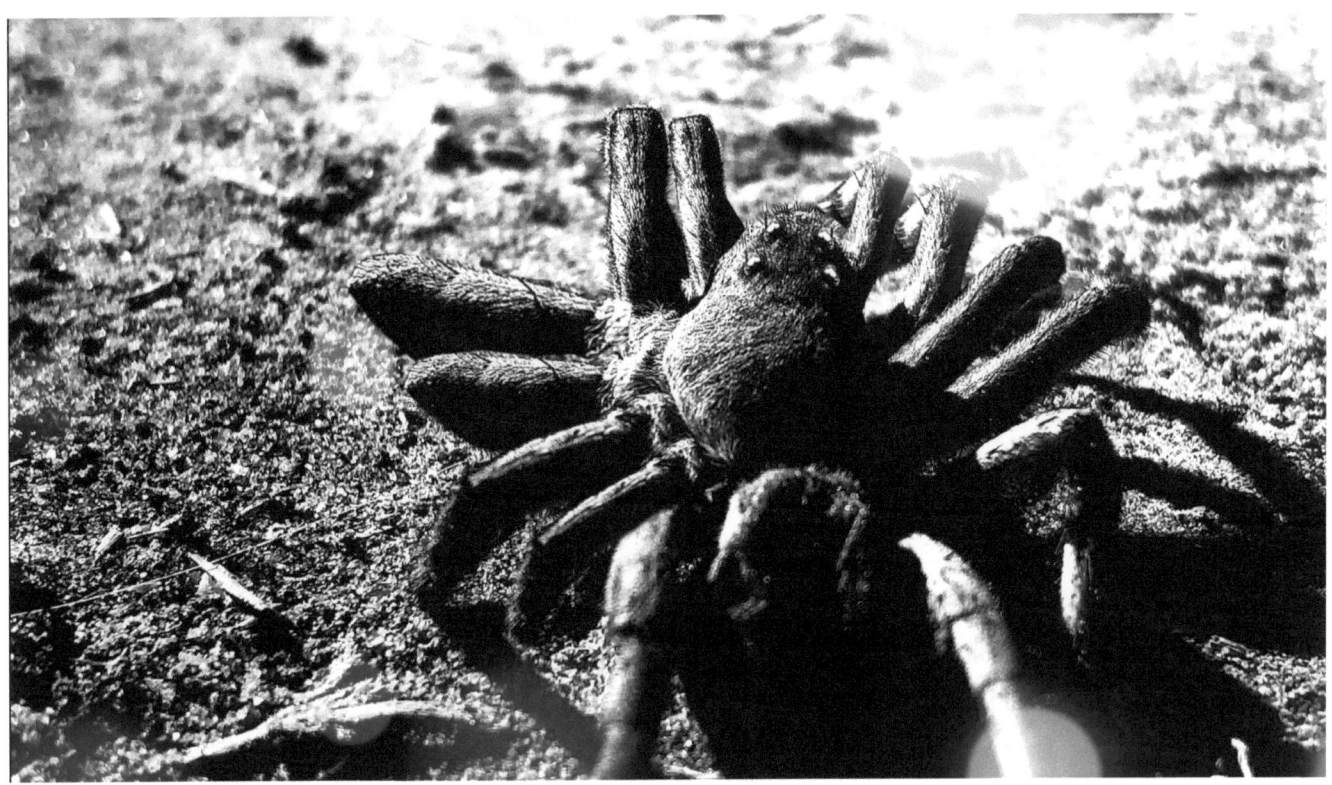

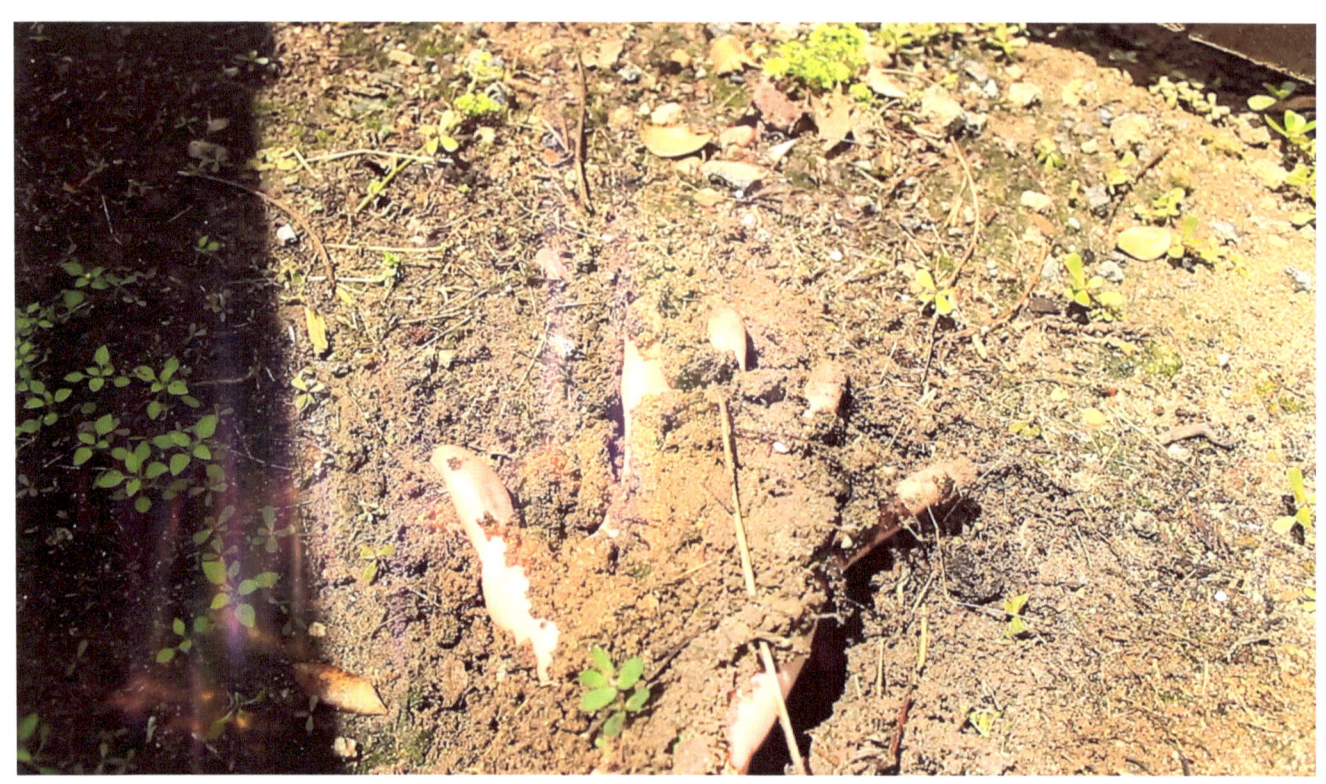

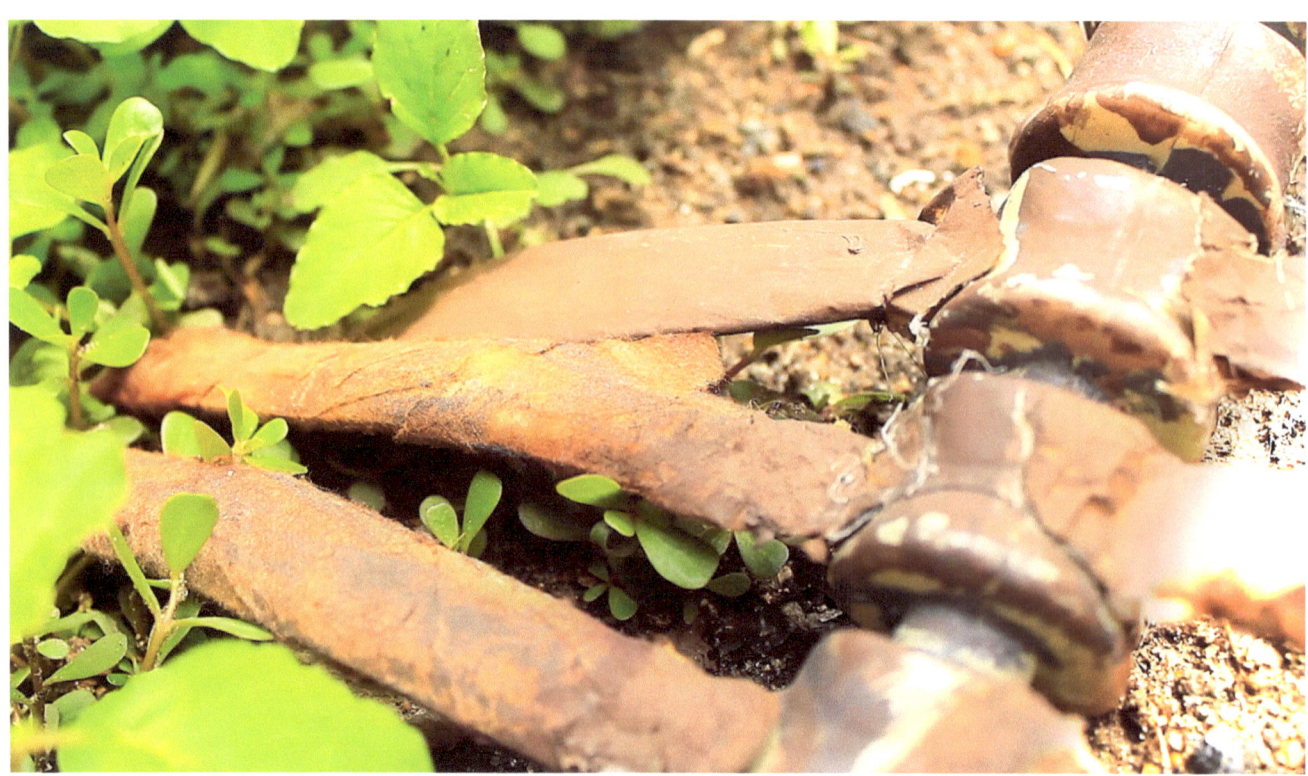

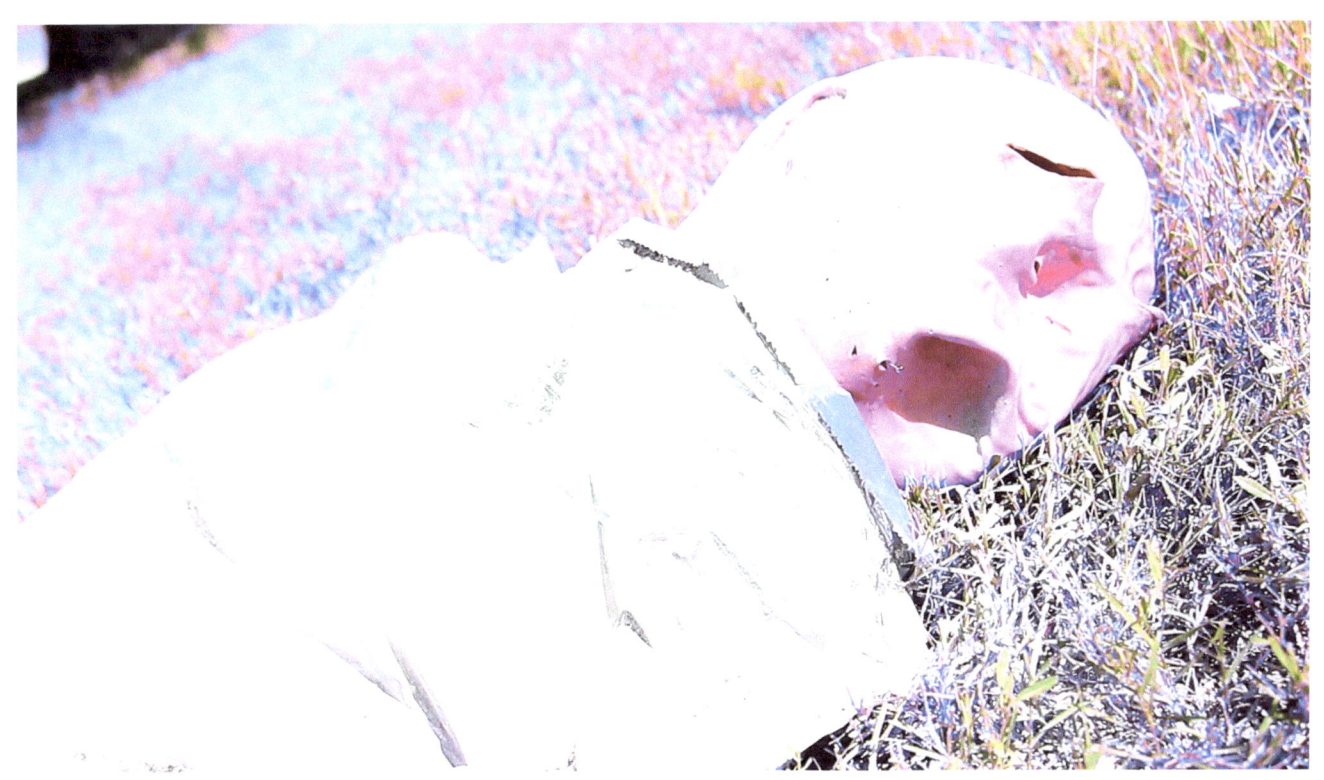

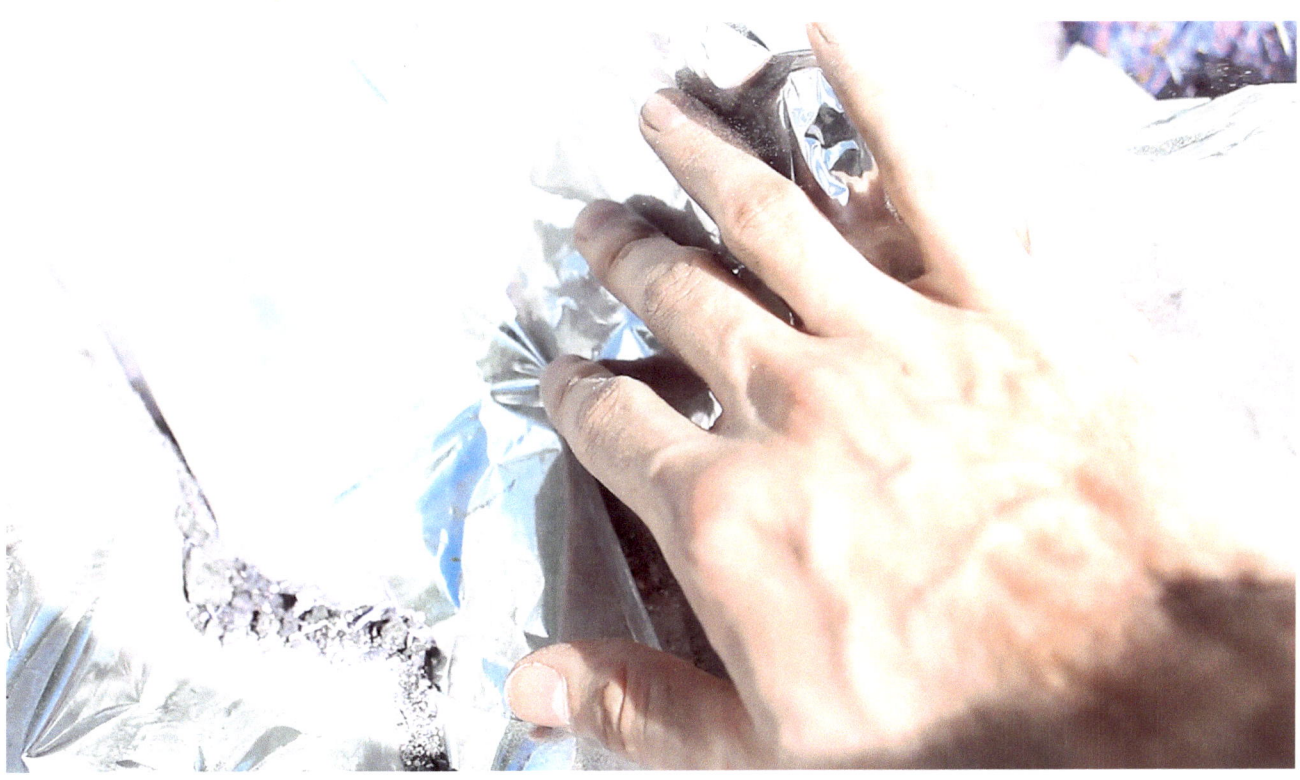

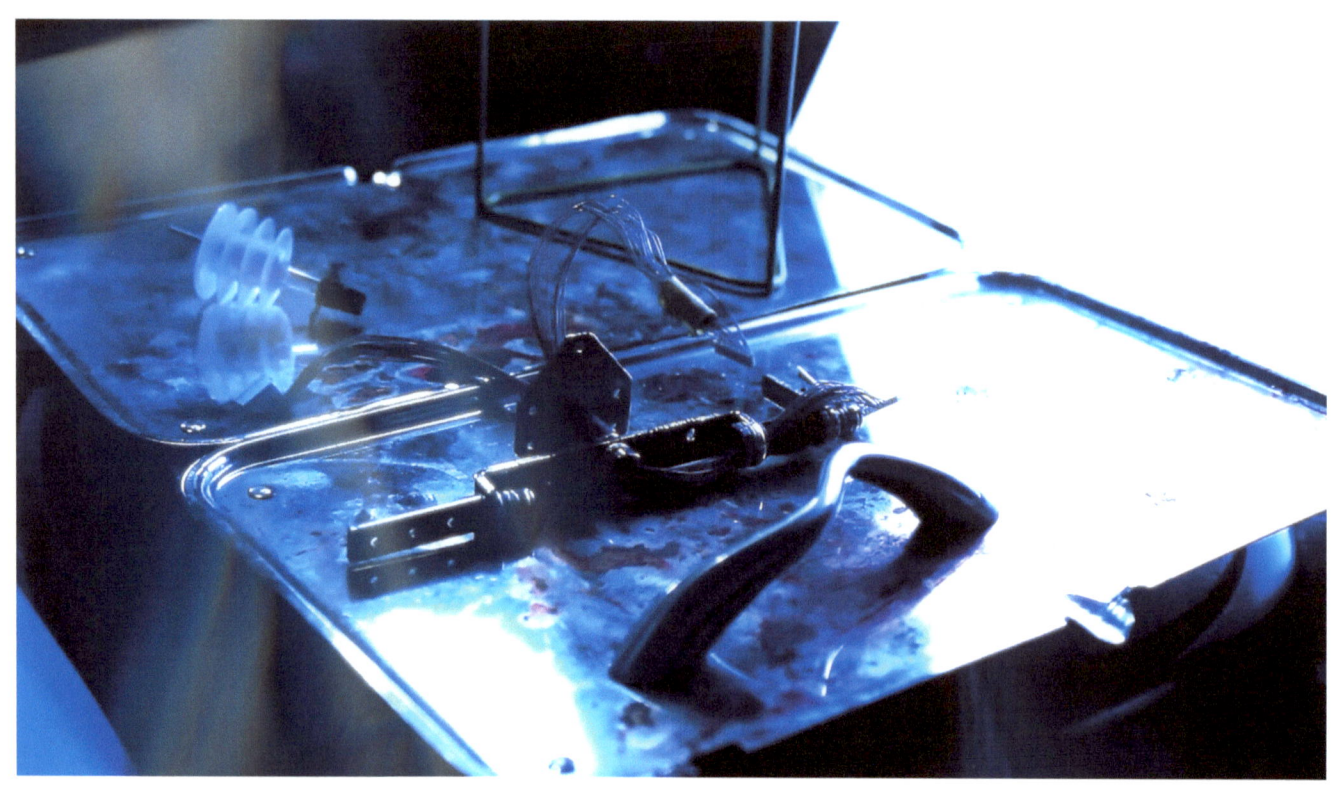

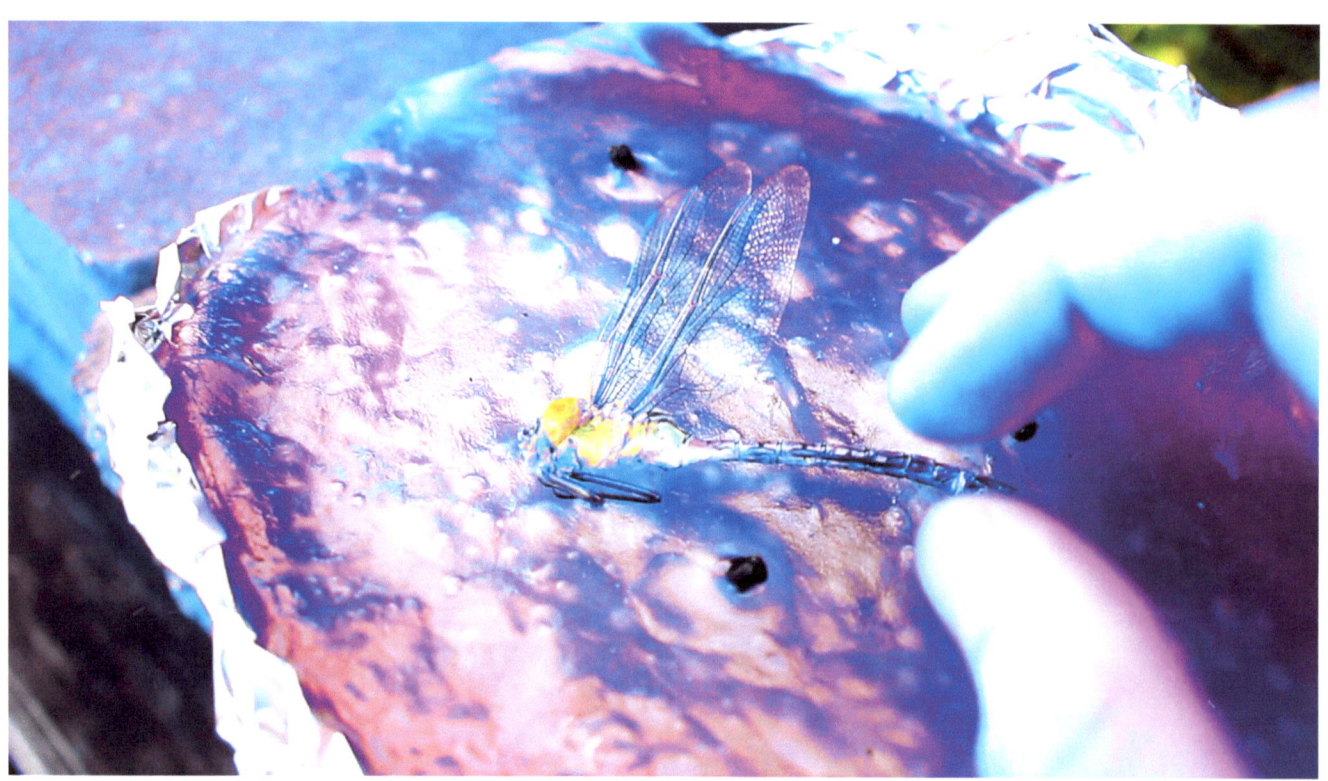

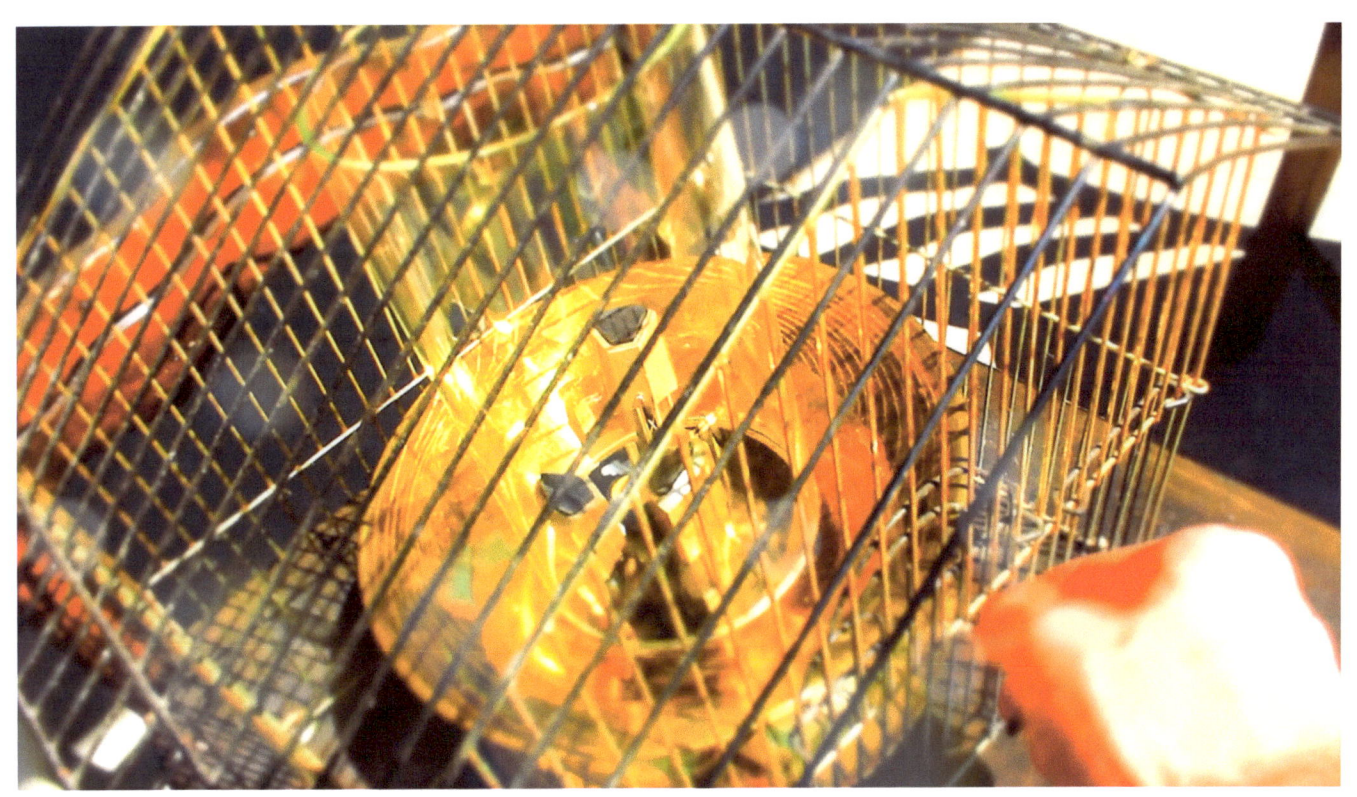

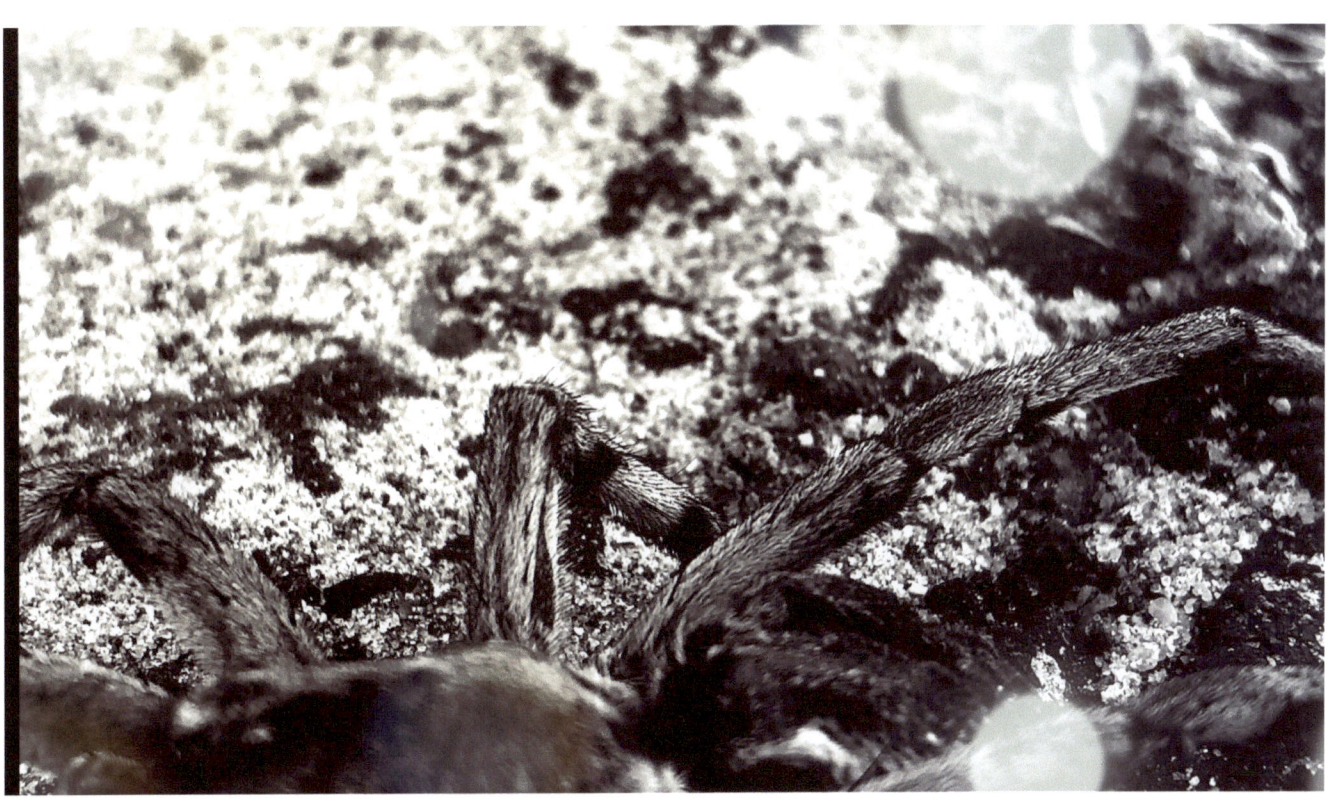

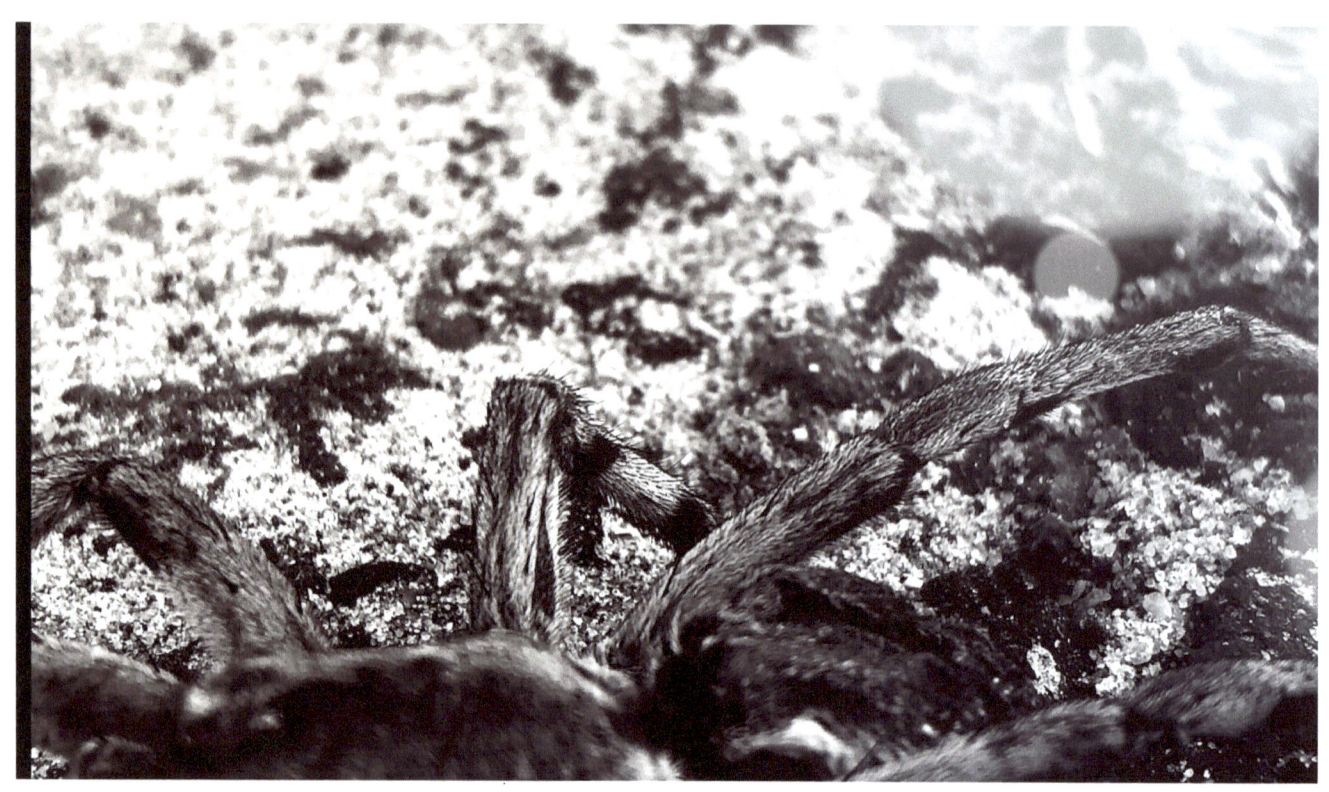

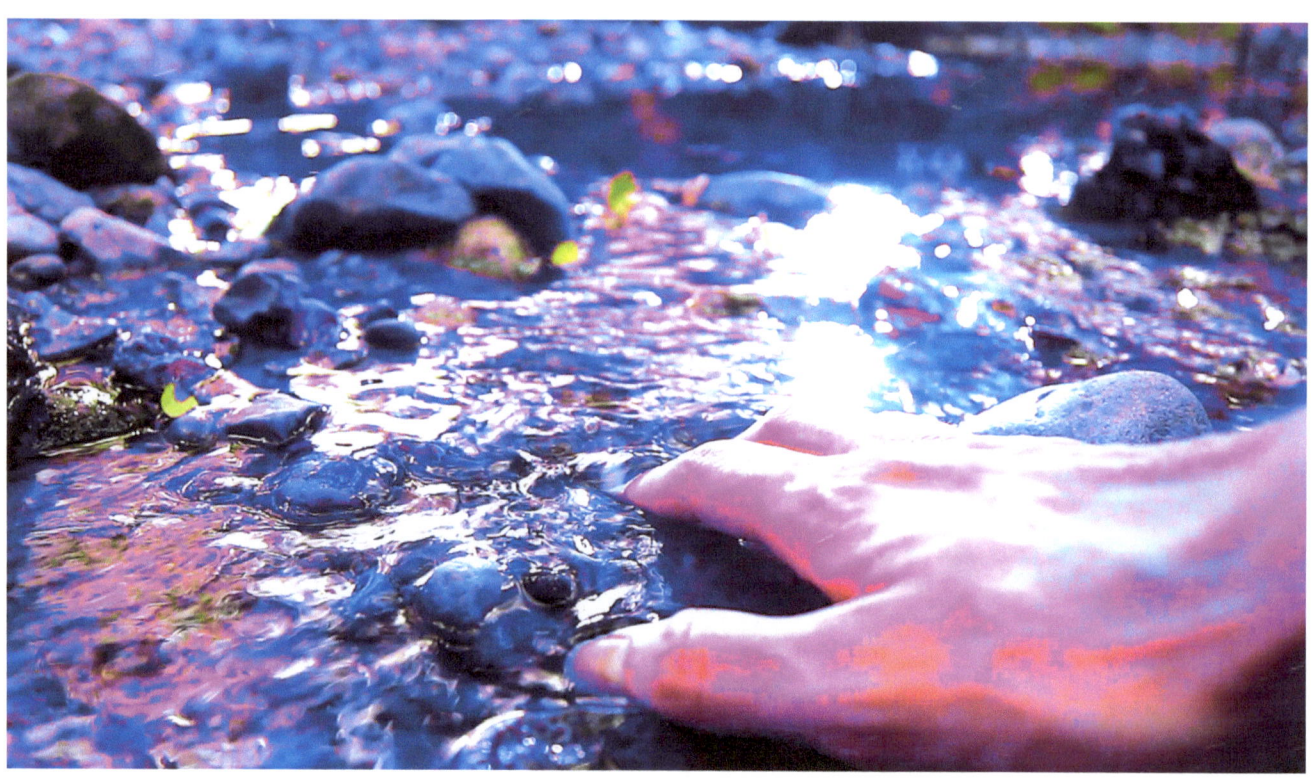

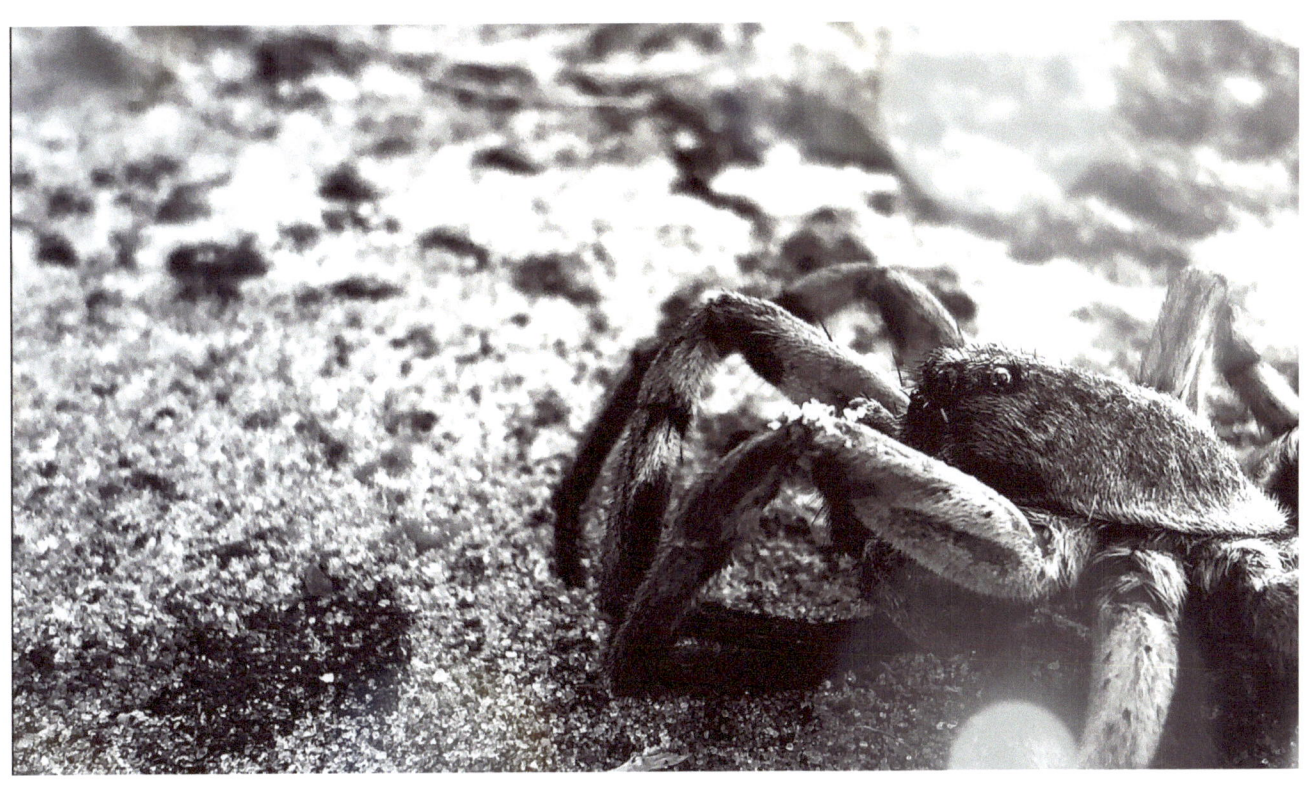

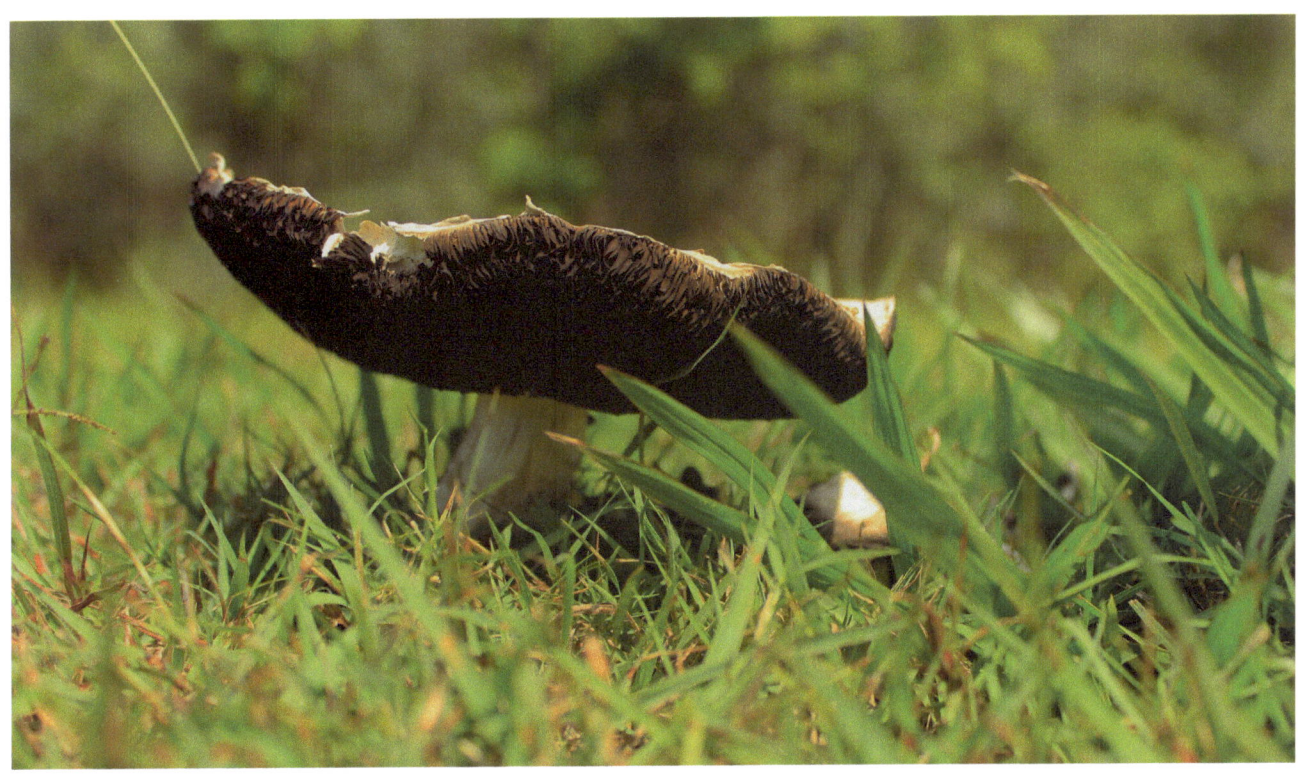

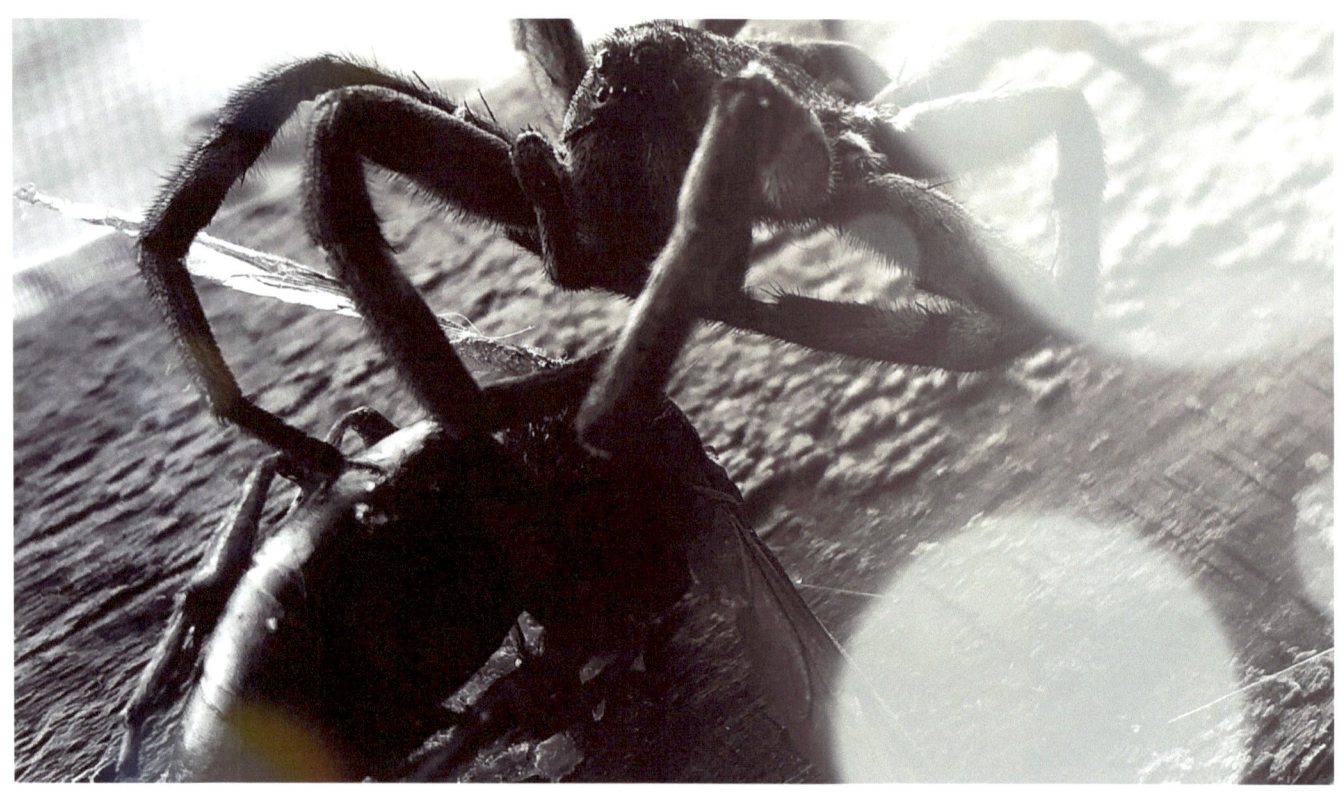

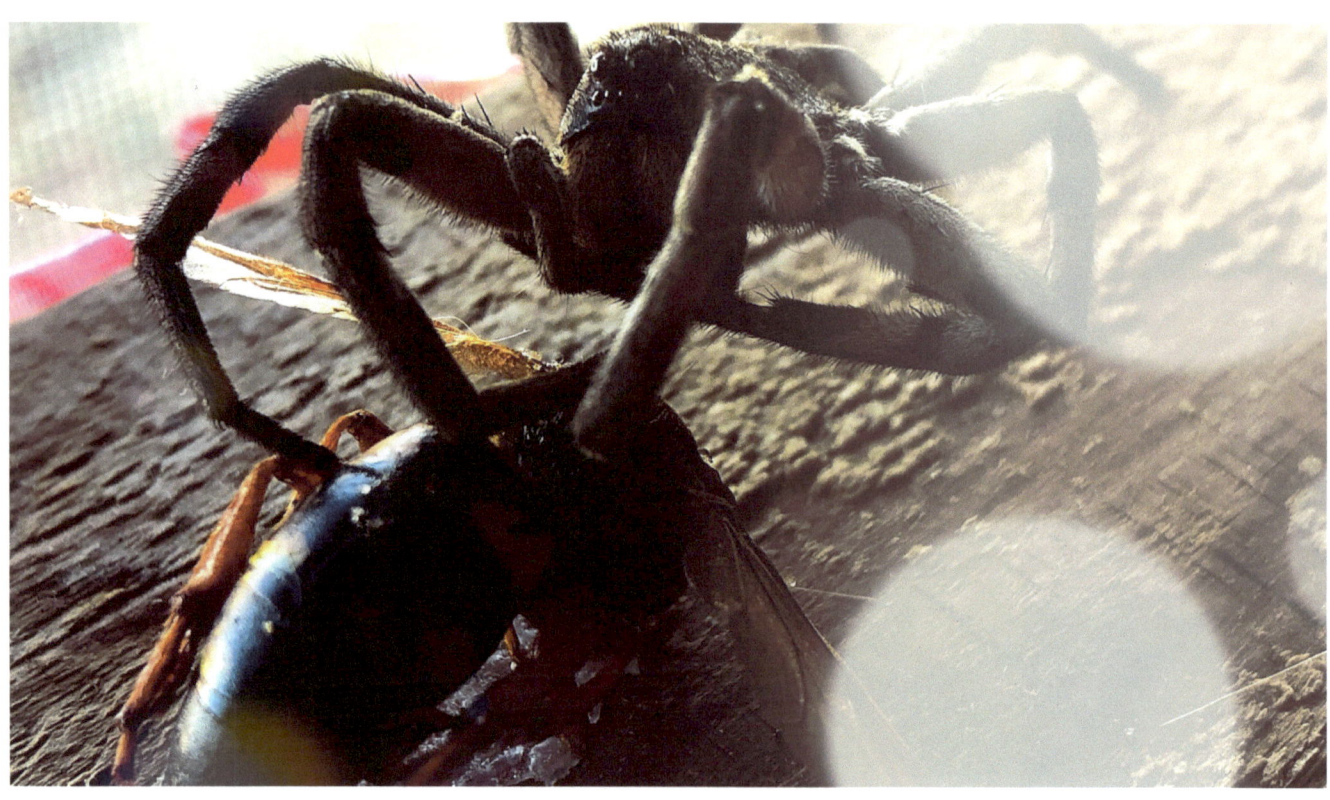

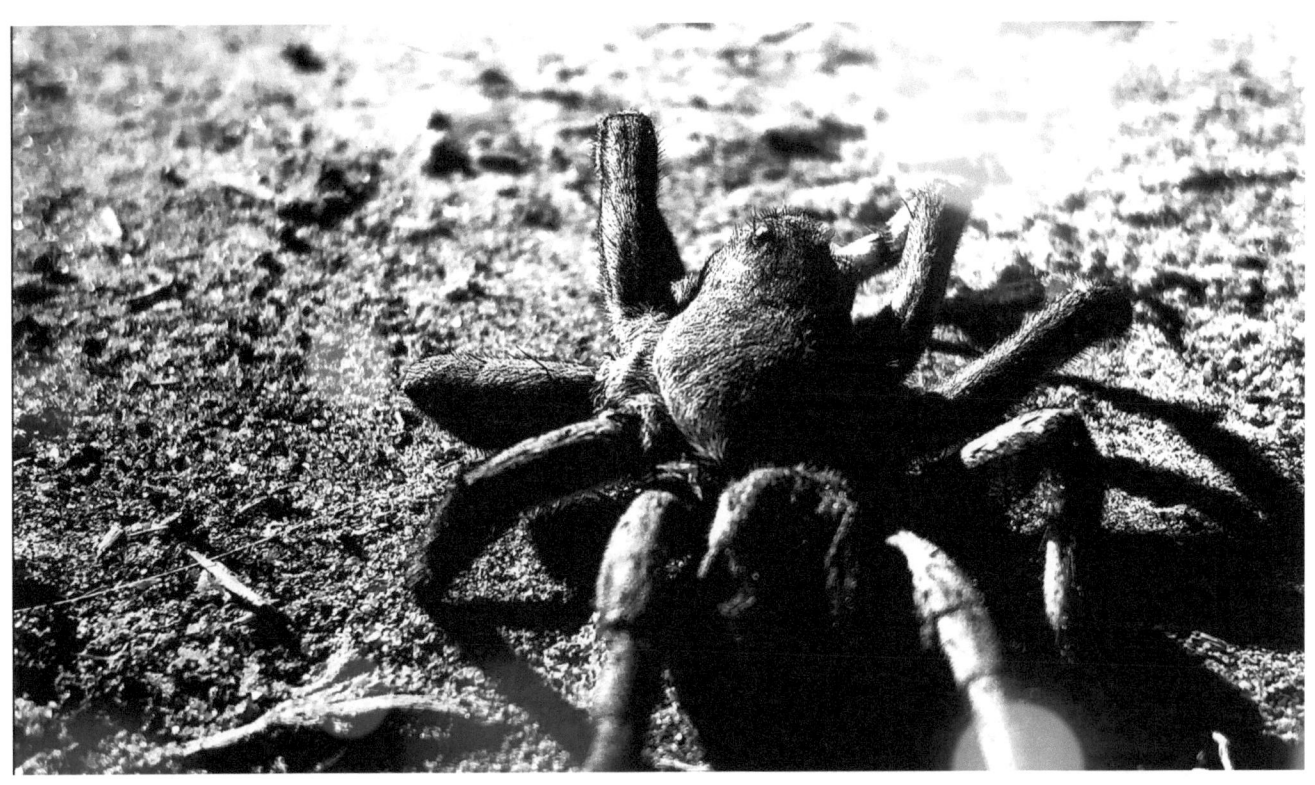

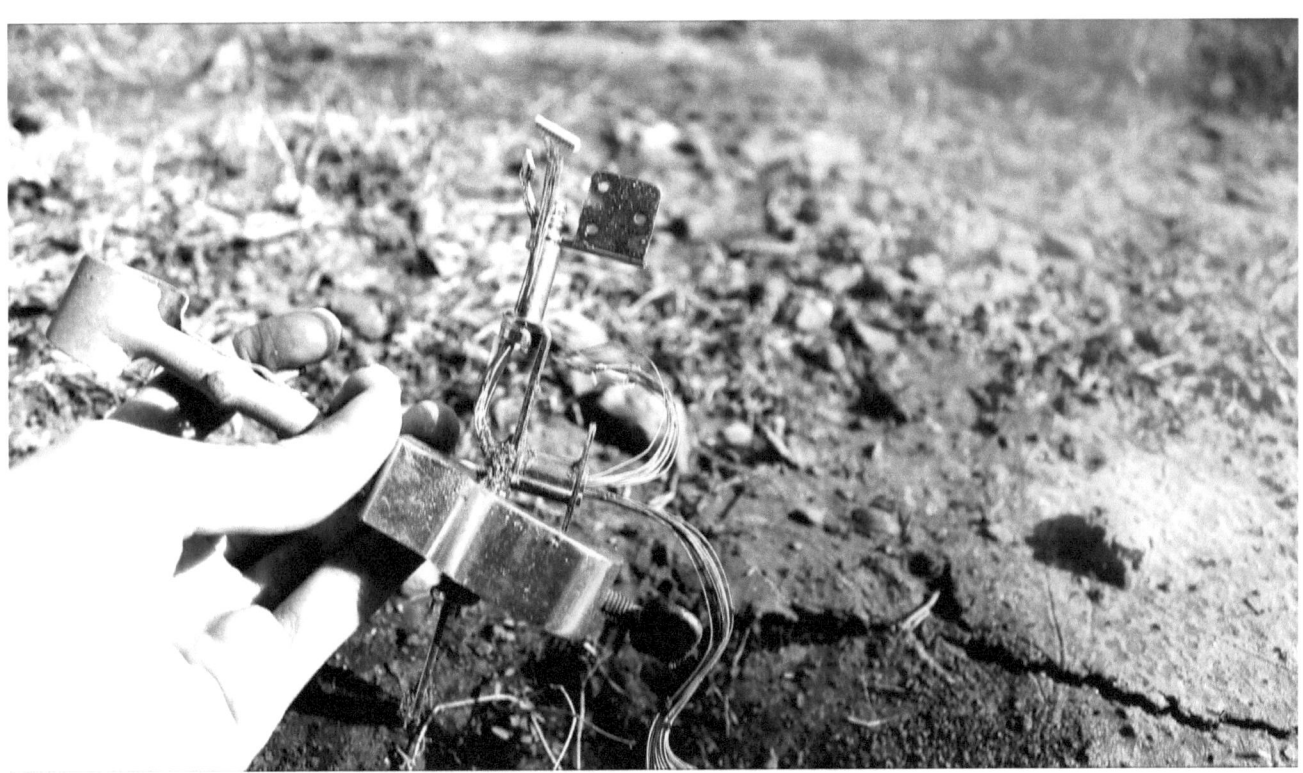

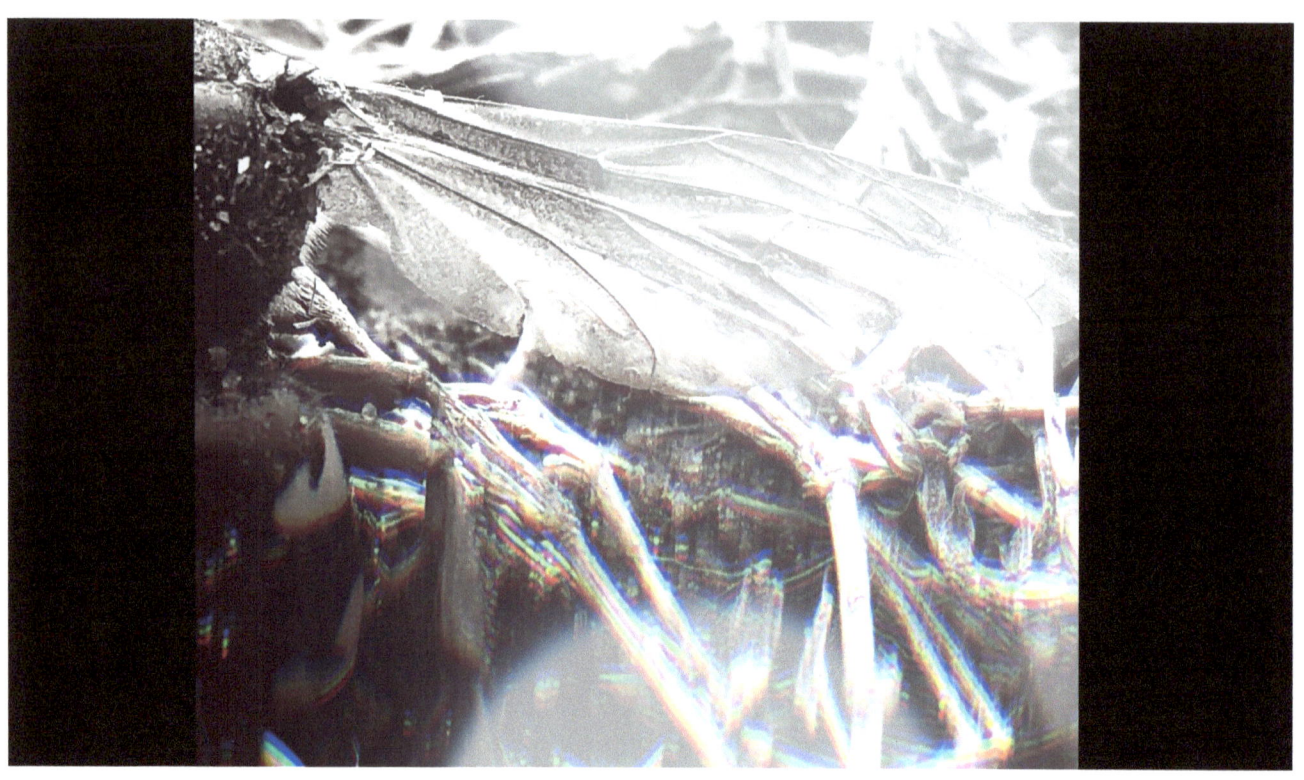

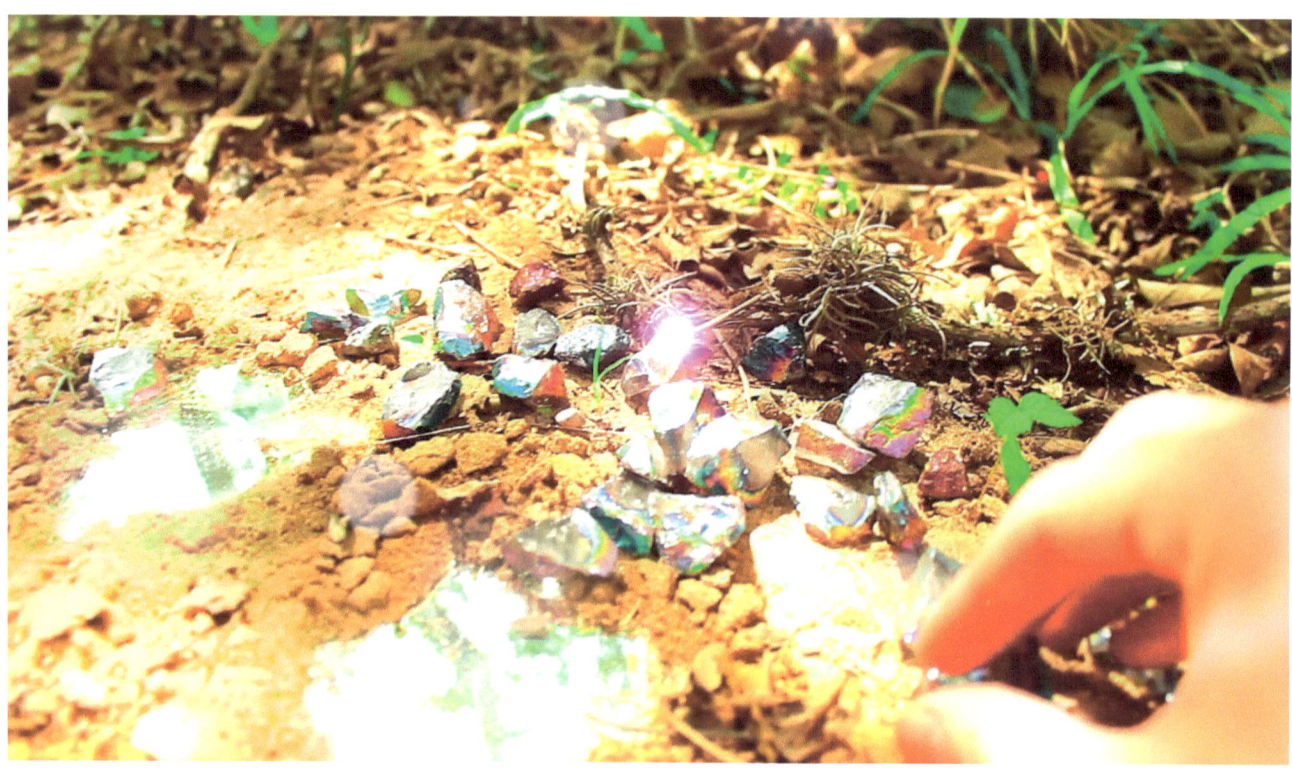

Illusions.

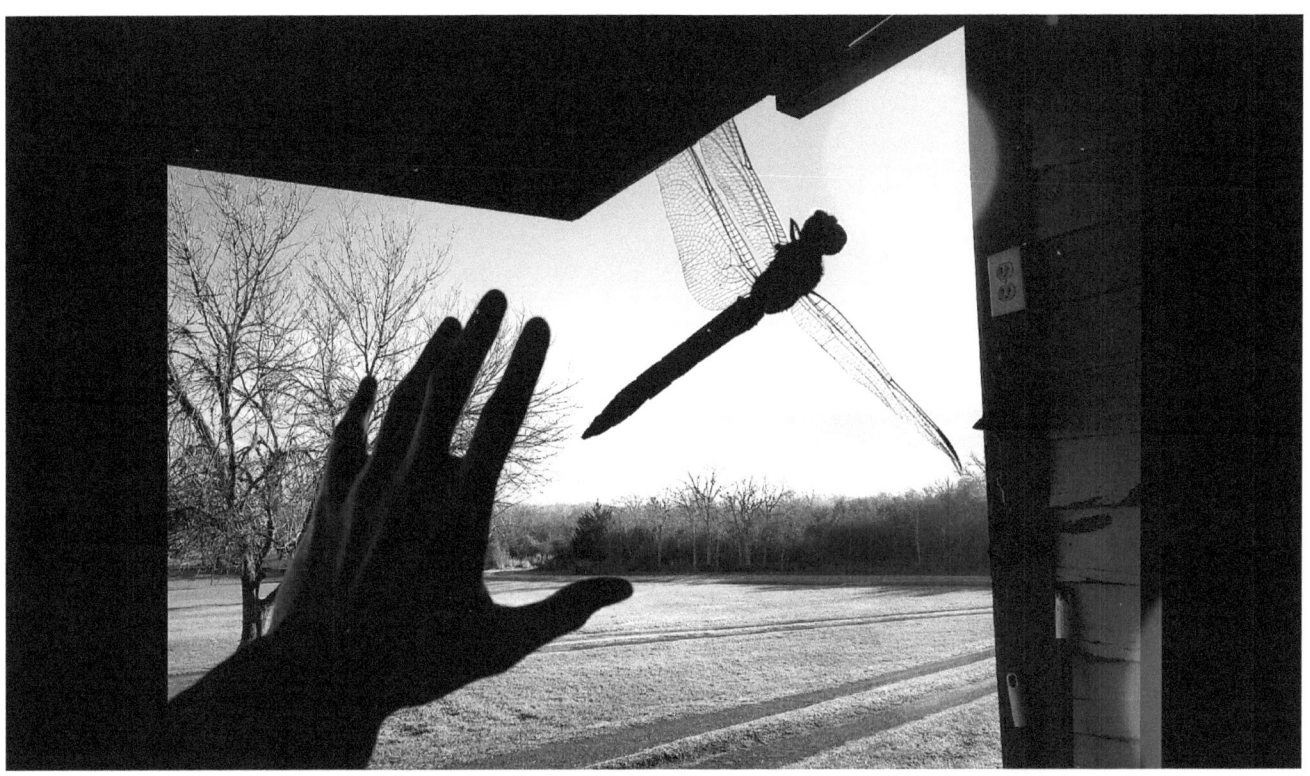

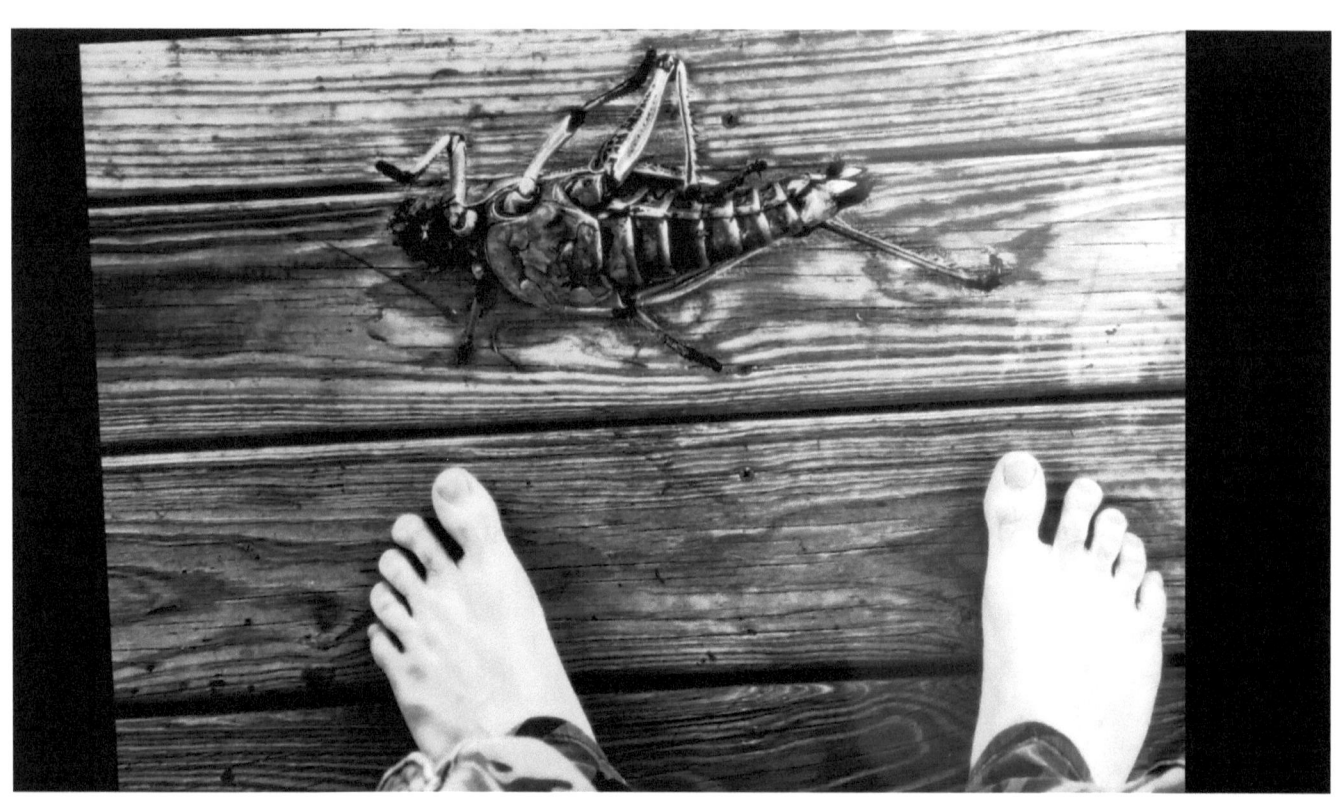

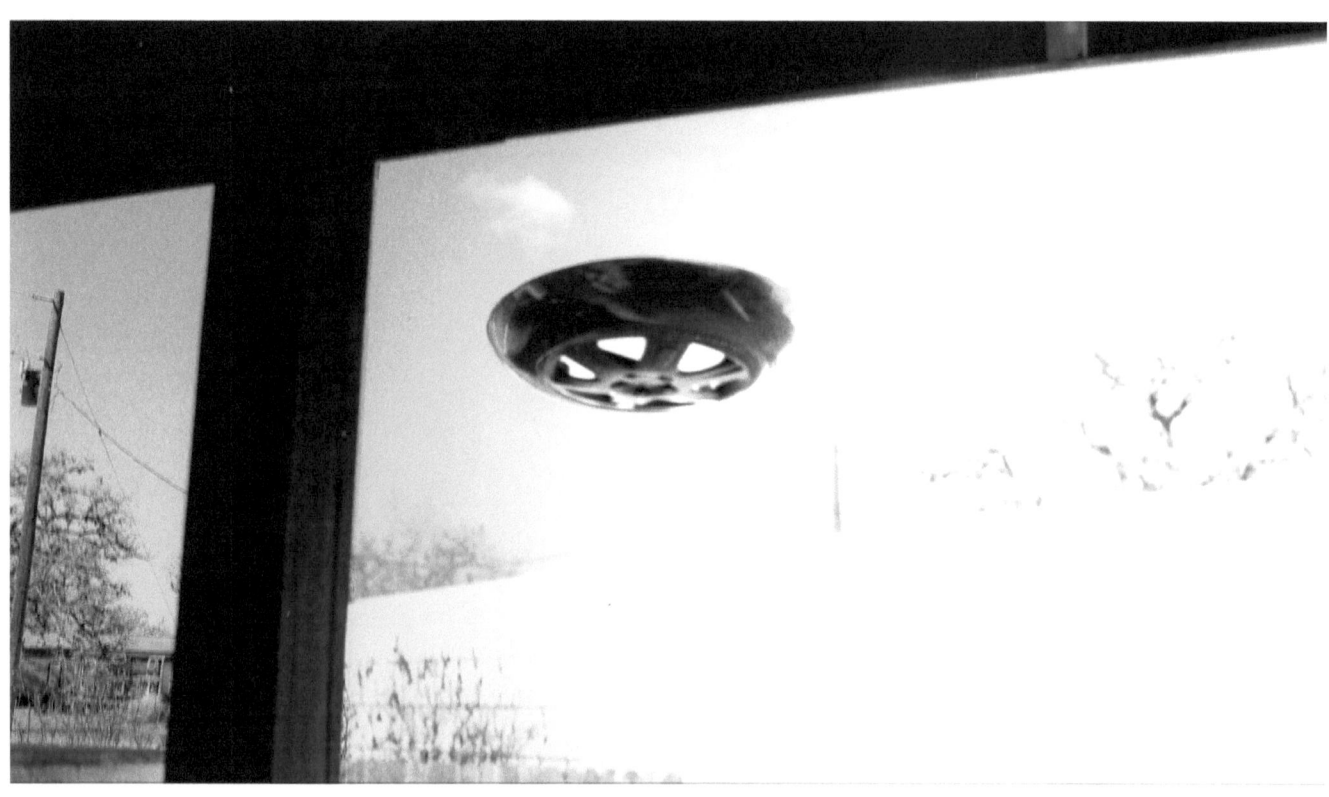

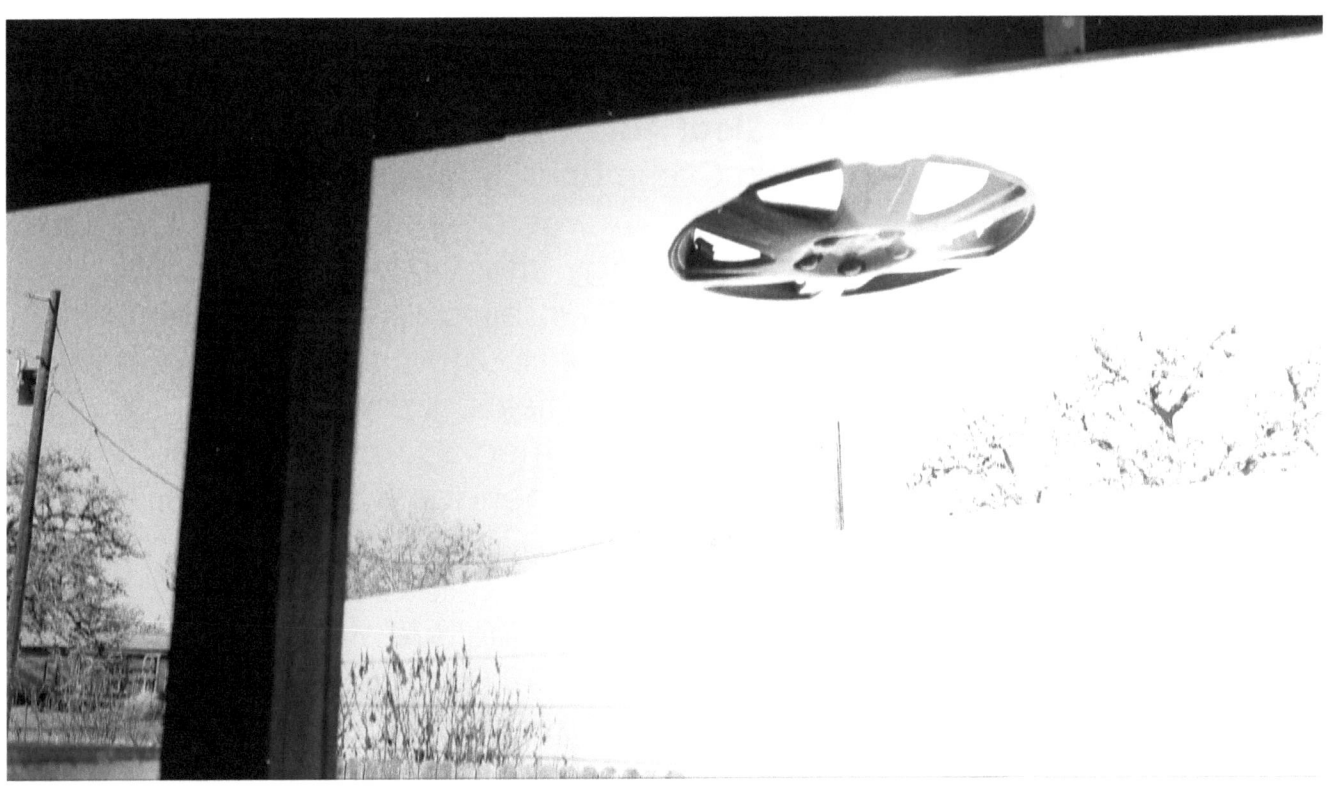

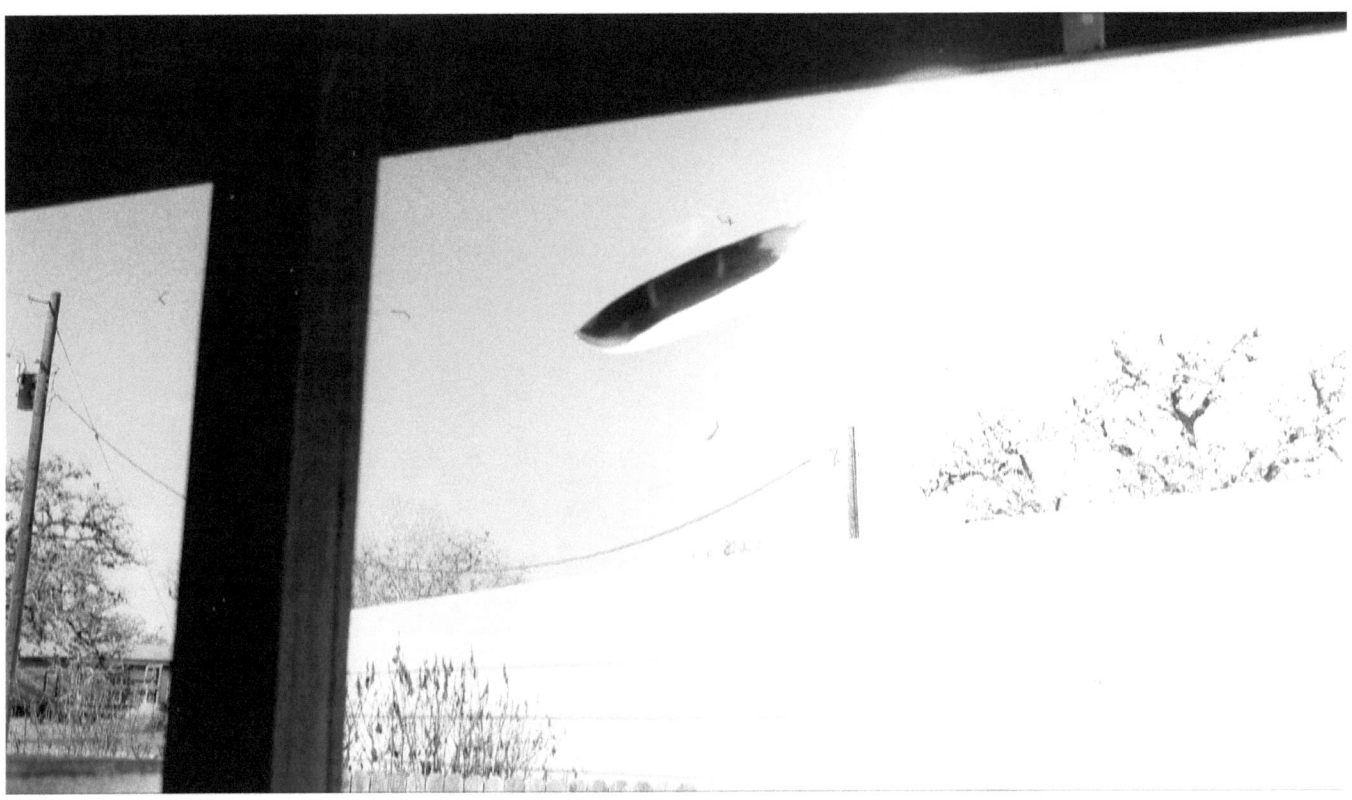

About the Author

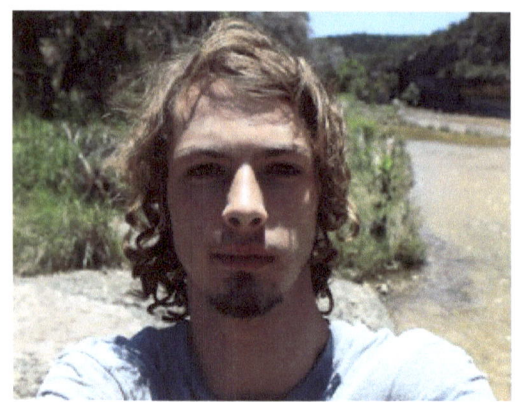

Steal Adcock, M.A., LPC earned his B.A. in Communication Studies at St. Mary's University where he also minored in Psychology after which he earned his M.A. in Counseling Psychology at the University of Houston-Victoria. Steal has studied the fields of psychology, philosophy, theology, and physics. He is also an independent filmmaker, surrealist oil painter, published researcher for scientific journals, and lucid dreamer. His previous publications include: *My Dreams, Nightmares, and Lucid Dreams Collection: Hundreds of Dreams Shared from My Dream Journals.*

Check out his other books:

My Dreams, Nightmares, And Lucid Dreams Collection: Hundreds Of Dreams Shared From My Dream Journals (2024).

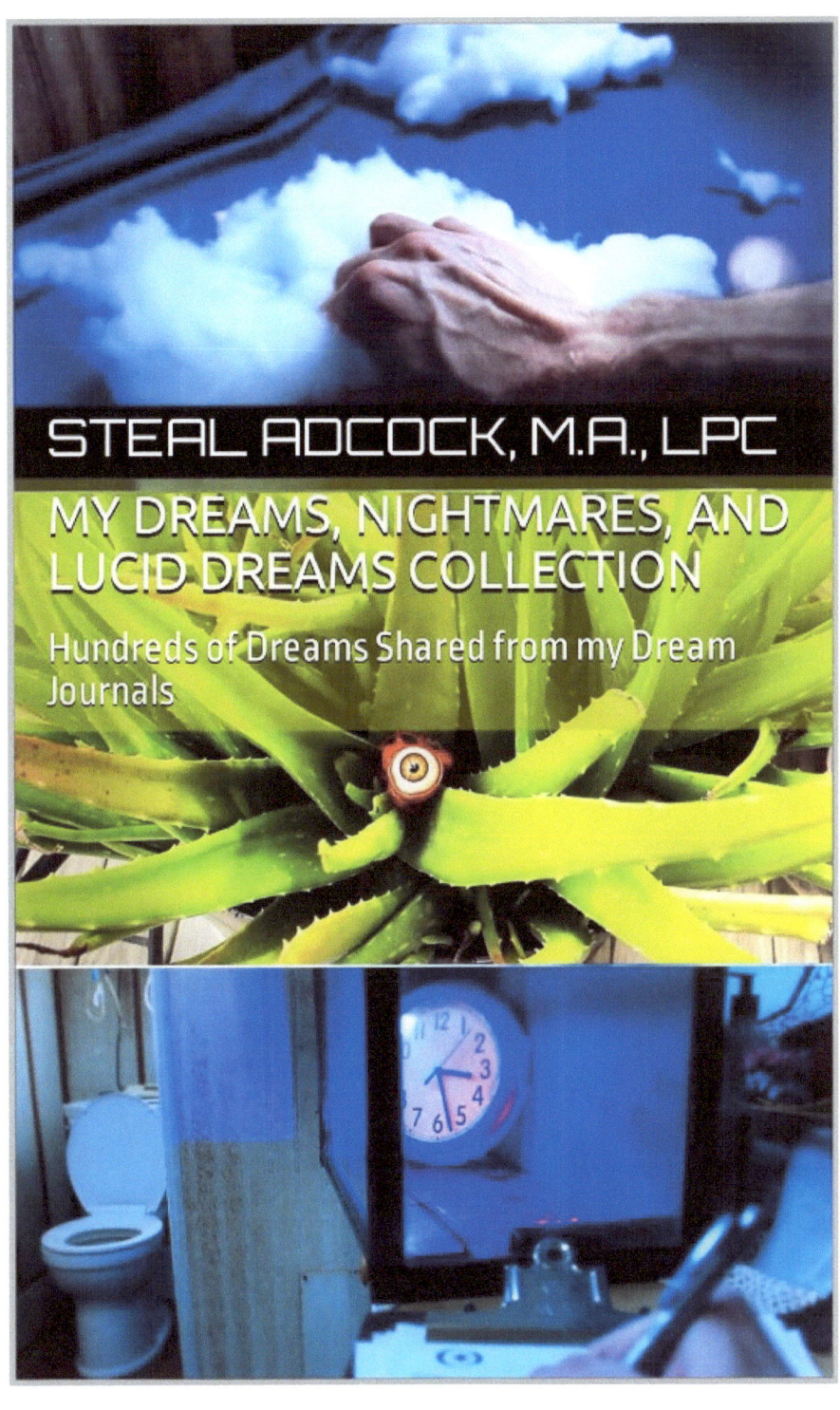